Love Letters from Heaven

by

Terri F. Williams

Much Success

Published by Mrs. Bea's Publishing

This is a work of non-fiction. All scripture references have been taken from the King James Version of the Bible (KJV), the New International Version (NIV) and the Amplified Bible (AMP).

First Print December 2009
Printed in the United States of America

Cover Illustration: Lisa L. Sims
Editor: Linda J. Wilson

ISBN: **978-0-9825821-0-7**

Dedication

For my Lord and Savior Jesus Christ, the only true God.

CONTENTS

Prayer for the Lost

Dear God,

I give you all the praise and honor for this spoken word you have put in my heart. I pray God that you will bless this book. Lead it into the hands of those that need a word of encouragement from you. Let it find its way into the hands of the lonely, the brokenhearted, the lost, and especially to the person that needs a word from you, God. I believe by faith that anyone who reads **Love Letters from Heaven** will be blessed and encouraged.

Please bless the lost, open the eyes of the blind so they too can see the truth. Teach us dear God to love one another as you love us. Help our weaknesses and strengthen our faith in you. I give you all the praise, all the honor, and all the glory for the birthing of this book.

In closing, God, I ask that you teach us how to forgive one another, and remind us daily that there is nothing in the world greater than the power of your love. I pray all these things in the name of your dear son, Jesus Christ. Amen.

Sincerely,

Terri F. Williams

Preface

- The Spirit of the Lord is upon me, because he hath anointed me to preach the gospel to the poor; he hath sent me to heal the brokenhearted, to preach deliverance to the captives, and recovering of sight to the blind, to set at liberty them that are bruised. — *Luke 4:18 (KJV)*

Within the pages of this book, I will not only share the spoken word of God, but also testimonies from my own life. If seeing is truly believing, then look and see what the Lord has done for me.

I have lived my life like an open book. My eyes see poetry and beauty when I look at the things that God has created. When I was a child I knew God had a purpose for my life. Unlike most children, I could feel other people's pain. I can recall being as young as ten years old, and on one particular day while on my way to school I saw a small bird lying dead on the sidewalk. Children walking past hissed and sneered as they commented on how dirty and filthy the bird was. As I looked at the lifeless fowl, my heart melted inside. I thought of how a life had been lost, and how terrible it was that nobody cared.

I knelt down beside him and cuffed him in the palm of my hand as tears rolled down the sides of my face. Without another thought, I headed back home and went to the backyard where I rested the bird on the ground. Just across the yard was a large tree with broken branches laying underneath it. I picked up a sturdy branch and began digging a shallow grave. As I continued to dig, tears constantly fell from my eyes. Gently, I laid his body in the grave and then got on my knees and said a prayer.

As I looked on with compassion at the tiny creature that once filled God's beautiful sky, I began to see more of God's love. At that moment I realized there was a softness inside of me that other kids didn't have, a softness that would be crushed time and time again, by cruel people who had no idea what it really meant to be loved.

Like the small bird that lay on the sidewalk, we too need the Lord's compassion when he sees us fall. He picks us up, dusts us off and gives us the love we need in order to go on. In my young mind, that was how I thought God saw man. Like birds, sometimes we fall from the sky wounded, but then he comes along and gives us the love we need so we can once again fill his world and spread the truth about his love.

As I grew older, I considered myself a female Jonah. I say this because I had spent many years of my life running from God. I knew I was different, but I did not want to be. I wanted to be popular and accepted by everyone. I did all I could to win the affection of people, never once asking God for any of his love. There were times when my life had bits and pieces of joy and happiness as the world gives it, but there was still a big void in my life. In my lifetime, I had shed many tears. Most of those tears fell because I felt incomplete. I cried not only for myself, but for people as well. I remembered the many people I had met along life's highway. God used many of those people to help and mold me into the woman I am today. I had been chosen, yet I was not ready to surrender to God. He had called me to do his will, but my own selfish desires combined with the fear of being considered a radical Christian kept me away. As the years began to pass, I became too busy doing my own thing, until the day God stepped in. He was preparing a whale for me, a whale that would one day vomit me back onto the shore like Jonah.

I have been in the operating room stretched out on a table at least four times in my life. I realized later, I could have avoided many of the things I suffered if I would have simply yielded to the voice of God. The Bible says that God chooses us. We try to take a little credit by thinking we chose him, but actually, he chooses us.

- Ye have not chosen me, but I have chosen you, and ordained you, that ye should go and bring forth fruit, and that your fruit should remain: that whatsoever ye shall ask of the Father in my name he may give it to you. — *John 15:16 (KJV)*

My present condition today: I have two metal rods in my left leg extending from my knee to my ankles. I later developed two large tumors as big as melons in my uterus. The tumors were intertwined so severely my uterus could not be saved. Years later, I developed a bad case of pneumonia that nearly took my life. And the last storm that came, left me without the full use of my right hand during a terrible accident.

I cried out to God and repented. Then the whale that held me captive inside his belly vomited me back onto the shore of the sea. It was then that I made a conscious decision to stop running from the Lord and do his will. My walk with the Lord had really taken flight, although there were times I fell along the way. Like I had compassion when I picked up that small bird, he picked me up and set me back on the path of righteousness.

I wrote this book because I wanted to reach people who were on the verge of giving up hope. People need to know that God is still in the miracle business, and he will not forget his children even when they stray. I share my testimonies with people in hopes that they will take heed when God is calling.

There is a scripture in Psalm 91:1 that is a prayer of protection. All my life I never knew what Psalm 91:1 was really saying until God gave me a revelation, which I will share with you.

Please understand this one thing: The devil is real, and he does not want to play with you. He wants to kill you! I want to give you a revelation that you have probably never thought about, and I pray your heart will be open to receive it.

Love Letters from Heaven was written to inspire and encourage you. Inside you will find a lot of good information that will bless you. I realize that for some people the Bible can be intimidating. Many of the biblical words might appear hard to understand, especially as a new Christian. I have included some of my personal experiences and combined them with the word of God and thus *Love Letters from Heaven* was born.

Before I wrote this book, I honestly prayed and asked God for the wisdom to write it. I pray it will bless you and help you with your walk with the Lord. Read the stories repeatedly until you get the full understanding of its meaning. Learn from some of my experiences. Do not allow your heart to become stubborn, proud, shallow and unwilling to take heed to God's word. He is always there and he has promised to never leave you or forsake you.

Stand in the Shadow of the Almighty

Remember . . .

- He that "dwelleth" in the secret place of the most High shall remain under the "shadow" of the Almighty. — *Psalm 91:1 (KJV)*

The Bible says that Jesus is the light of the world. Can anything cast a shadow without light? Casting a shadow without light is impossible. Jesus is like a candle in the hands of God. While God stands holding the candle (which is Jesus) his shadow is cast on the wall or ground. God said in his word that he (meaning anyone) that dwelleth in the secret place of the Most High *shall* abide under the *shadow* of the Almighty." This secret place that God is speaking of is found only in him. It is when we are resting in him, hidden beneath his wings, is where we find safety . . . Jesus's presence causes God's shadow to appear. Jesus is the *light* of the world! He stands between God and man. As long as we "dwell" in the secret place, we shall "remain" under the shadow (protection) of the Almighty.

As I look back on the tragedies that have occurred in my own life, I was not standing in God's shadow. Like a lost sheep, I strayed from the flock. After I walked away, the devil spotted me wandering all alone. He knew my umbrella of protection was gone, and he took the opportunity and attacked my body at every turn.

During the times when I was standing in the shadow, he could not reach me. Therefore, I will tell you once again, there is safety in the shadow of the Almighty. Satan tries to get us to step outside the will of God. He knows that when we walk in rebellion of God's laws, we open the door for sin to come in. Satan can cause many tragedies in the life of man. He did it to Job. However, the best part about tragedies is, like Job, God can turn those tragedies into miracles!

- And we know that all things work together for good to them that love God, to them who are the called according to *his* purpose. — *Romans 8:28 (KJV)*

I know that God will get his glory no matter what the enemy does. As you read this book and adhere to the advice I have written, I pray that my words will take root in your heart when you feel compelled to step outside the shadow of the Almighty.

To avoid any confusion, I will first share with you the things that tempted me to step outside of the shadow. My prayer is to win souls for Christ and to touch someone's life. No matter what obstacles life brings your way, remember dear one, stay in the shadow of the Almighty.

May the Lord God keep and bless you.

Acknowledgments

Special thanks to Prophet Dennis Cramer, who in his obedience brought me the word of God. Thank you to the Heart of Jesus Church, pastor and Prophet Cedric Banks and his wife, Prophetess Donetta Banks for your prayers, and the prophetic words you have spoken over my life. You both have been obedient to the Lord by preaching God's word of truth and for that I am eternally grateful. The television ministries have allowed us to hear and see great men and women of God. They have had a vast impact on my life because of their dedication to the ministry. I can only hope and pray that someday God will use me as he has used others to further the gospel of Jesus Christ.

To the angels God sent to me when I was sick and could not care for myself: Valerie Webb, Shanae Tatum, Maxine Thompson, Viginia Watts, & Elina Cobb.

Letter One
Milk or Meat?

As the body needs food to survive, likewise the spiritual man needs food to grow. We cannot feed the spiritual man the same food that we feed our physical bodies. In order for our spiritual man to grow, we must feed him the word of God.

People can be "saved" for years and they still cannot digest meat. Like babies, they are still on the bottle. When we first come to Christ we are all like babies in need of a bottle. God, being the merciful father that he is, feeds us milk, because he knows we are not yet strong enough to eat meat. How much we grow and how fast we grow are the result of our decisions. God is not going to cram his word down our throats. He gave man something that he did not give the animals; he gave man a will.

I remember a time when I was very worldly. I had many friends who attended church every Sunday, yet they could not quote a simple scripture. On the weekends, my friends and I used to hang out and party until dawn. If you were to listen to us conversing, you would not be able to distinguish between the Christian and the sinner.

The year that the Lord saved me, I began studying the Bible intensely. The more I studied, the stronger I became in the word. In a matter of time, I had soon surpassed those same friends who had been in the church for years. They were astounded as I quoted scriptures and explained their meaning. Oftentimes I would have to stop and explain a scripture as they looked at me dazed and confused. However, I was troubled in my spirit. Why didn't they understand God's word like I did? It was not until I received a revelation from God that the answer came.

- But the natural man receiveth not the things of the Spirit of God: for they are foolishness unto him: neither can he know them, because they are spiritually discerned. — *1 Corinthians 2:14 (KJV)*

While in college, I attended a small church located in Tennessee. I can recall the pastor of the church at the time, and how much he loved sharing the word of God. Many of the college kids attended the church regularly because the members showed us so much love. There were times when the pastor stepped on quite a few toes during his sermons. He did not have a problem telling people the truth according to the word of God. He would often say he would rather obey God than please man. I was very fortunate to sit under his teachings. He was a faithful man and believed in teaching the word of God.

Our church was anything but routine. Oftentimes the pastor would say, "I don't know what the Lord is going to do this morning, but no matter what he does, we're going to be obedient to the spirit of the Lord, and let him have his way."

I attended Bible study regularly, and my prayer life was increasing at an incredible speed! Slowly, I began witnessing in the streets along with other believers. I had finally grown strong enough to eat a little meat.

I also loved and still do love to hear Christians singing in the spirit. When a Christian sings in the spirit,

2

the Holy Spirit allows them to sing in another language. If you have never heard them sing, you should go to a church where believers are singing in the spirit. It is awesome to hear.

God gives a believer many gifts. Unfortunately, many of the gifts he gives us are simply not used. One of the gifts that I was particularly interested in was the gift of speaking in tongues.

- But the manifestation of the spirit is given to every man to profit withal.

- For to one is given by the Spirit the word of wisdom; to another the word of knowledge by the same Spirit;

- To another faith by the same Spirit; to another the gifts of healing by the same Spirit;

- To another the working of miracles; to another prophecy; to another discerning of spirits; to another *divers* kinds of tongues; **to another the interpretation of tongues**:

- But all these worketh that one and the selfsame Spirit, dividing to every man severally as he will.
  — *1 Corinthians 12:7-11 (KJV)*

It is important to remember that when we are in the Assembly of God (church), and someone stands up and begins speaking in an unknown tongue, that there should always be someone there to interpret what the speaker has said. If not, as the Bible says:

- If therefore the whole church be come together into one place, and all speak with tongues, and there come *in* those that are unlearned, or unbelievers, will they not say that ye are mad? — *1 Corinthians 14:23 (KJV)*

Paul said, ". . . for **greater is he that prophesieth** than he that speaketh with tongues, except he interpret, **that the church may receive edifying**." — *1 Corinthians 14:5 (KJV)*

During that time in my life, I did not fully understand the many gifts of the spirit. I wanted to learn how to speak in tongues. I learned through God's word that the Holy Spirit was someone I needed in regards to my prayer life. I still did not fully understand who the Holy Spirit was, or how to pray in the spirit.

- For he that speaketh in an **unknown tongue** speaketh not unto men, but unto God . . . howbeit **in the spirit** he speaketh mysteries. — *1 Corinthians 14:2 (KJV)*

Paul further stated, "Praying always with all prayer and supplication **in the spirit** . . ." — *Ephesians 6:18 (KJV)*

- Likewise the Spirit also helpeth our infirmities: for we know not what we should pray for as we ought: but the Spirit itself maketh intercession for us with groanings which cannot be uttered.

- And he that searcheth the hearts knoweth what is the mind of the Spirit, because he maketh intersession for the saints according to the will of God. — *Romans 8:26-27 (KJV)*

- And thou, Solomon my son, know thou the
  God of thy father, and serve him with a perfect
  heart and with a willing mind: **for the Lord
  searcheth all hearts, and understandeth all
  the imaginations of the thoughts:**
  — *1 Chronicles 28:9 (KJV)*

I spoke to my pastor about my concerns. He explained that receiving the Holy Spirit was not complicated; the only thing I had to do was ask.

One night during one of my studies, I took time to pray. I followed the pastor's instructions and asked God for the gift of the Holy Spirit. After I asked, I began to praise him. Although I could not speak in tongues, I knew how to praise God. I yielded my voice and began thanking him for everything in my life. Suddenly, the spirit gave unction to my voice, and my words began to flow in an unknown tongue. I could feel the warmth of the spirit filling me as I prayed to God.

Speaking in tongues was awesome! The morning could not come fast enough. I had to tell the pastor what had happened to me. He was happy for me, and further told me that praying in the Spirit was considered perfect prayer. We as believers do not know what to pray for, but the Holy Spirit knows exactly what we need. After that night, I began praying in the spirit every day.

When a person still drinks milk, he cannot understand spiritual things. I learned that you must use wisdom when witnessing to someone about the Lord. If you are not careful, you can actually choke a person with the word. No matter how much you want them to know the truth, they cannot understand. The best witness you have is your life. Be an example. We are like candles in a dark world.

Do not be deceived, God did not just save us to save us. He has a plan. We are supposed to be working in the vineyard (which is the world), winning souls for Christ, but unfortunately, many of us have been on milk for so long that we cannot help anyone because we do not ourselves know how to pray.

- When I was a child, I spake as a child, I understood as a child, I thought as a child: but when I became a man, I put away childish things.
  — *1 Corinthians 13:11 (KJV)*

Ask yourself and answer honestly. Are you the baby or the sitter? Milk or meat? The choice is up to you. Got milk?

Letter Two
Returning to the Vomit

I have heard some ministers say that God does not test us. I question that statement. Was it not God who told Abraham to sacrifice his beloved son, Isaac? Was that not a test? It might be old news, but I have news for you; eventually God is going to test you. When he does decide to test you, if you do not pass, you will be retaking the same test until you pass. There was a time when God was testing me. He was testing the one thing I struggled with the most, trusting in man. The Lord kept telling me in my spirit to trust him, not man, but I trusted man anyway and boy did I pay the price.

This test of trust lasted for what seemed like an eternity! I exchanged one situation for another, failing at every turn. But God was merciful, he kept creating new situations because he wanted me to learn to trust him. Ten years would pass before I would finally learn to trust God. He sent his word to me by his prophet. A man of God told me that the Lord said I had finally learned to trust in him.

I do not want to get ahead of myself. Before the word of the Lord came to me concerning trust, I endured many more trials in my life.

There are things you can expect to endure as a Christian, and those are tests and trials. Do not be discouraged, dear friend. Trials come to make you stronger and increase your faith. A positive note of encouragement is that God will allow a season of rest.

But soon afterwards, you will find yourself faced with yet another test or trial.

God was using these trials to strengthen my faith. After I had been serving the Lord for a year, I went through what some Christians refer to as a *dry spell*.

During a dry spell, it feels like somebody has pushed the pause button on your life. For me, it was like waiting to see the doctor. You know how they treat you at the doctor's office? You sit in the lobby and wait for your name to be called. After someone does decide to walk through the door and call your name, you feel a small sense of relief, although you know that you are being led to yet another room to simply wait. You wait, and wait and wait in that room for what seems like an eternity. You notice a few magazines on a table, which you flip through to occupy your mind. You glance at your watch, shake your head and wonder: When is the doctor going to come in and see about me?

That is how we treat God when it comes to waiting. We pray for something, and then the moment we get off our knees, we open our hand and expect God to move right away. When he does not move we become discouraged. Some people become so discouraged that they simply give up and walk out seeking another doctor. Their heart is set on finding a doctor who will not keep them waiting. They walk out on a doctor that has taken care of them and their family for years! These people grew impatient when the doctor did not show up when they expected him to.

That was like a dry spell for me, just waiting and waiting for something to happen. It seemed that God was being silent all of a sudden. In my mind, I did not think that he was answering my prayers, and to be honest there were days when I just did not "feel" so spiritual. I was becoming anxious as I stood watching worldly people doing whatever they wanted. All kinds of negative thoughts filled my mind, and within a span of time, feelings of greed and temptation began to manifest themselves. Unknowingly, I had foolishly opened the wrong door in my life, and the devil stepped right in.

Slowly, sin began to reign over me. Satan was subtly shooting arrow after arrow into my mind, practically taking charge of my every streaming thought. Daily, I was reminded of everything I did not have. My eyes were filled with the prosperity of people who did not know God, and showed no interest in knowing him. They were prospering while I waited. *How could this be?* I thought. *Why are the wicked prospering so much?* Even in your own life, you have seen it. I know you have. All you have to do is turn on the video channel and look at the big mansions and the expensive cars owned by some of the most wicked people I have ever seen. These people couldn't care less about serving God, they make jokes about him and his son day after day, and all they seemed to do in my eyes was prosper. I asked the Lord, "Why must this be?" It was then that my heart became hardened against the church. I wanted to have nice things, too. What was I doing wrong? During that point in my life, I did not understand the full knowledge of God's word. All I could see is what was before me. I took my Bible and hid it from my sight. I did not want to think of anything that reminded me of God. Perhaps he was punishing me for some sin I had not repented of. I knew in my heart that I was saved, according to the scriptures I had read in the Bible.

- That if thou shalt confess with thy mouth the Lord Jesus, and shalt believe in thine heart that God hath raised him from the dead, thou shalt be saved.

- For with the heart man believeth unto righteousness; and with the mouth confession is made unto salvation. — *Romans 10:9-10 (KJV)*

Within a matter of months, I began moving farther and farther away from God. I was now tired of going through tests and trials. My eyes had begun to focus on the things of this world, and I was taking notice of sinners at every turn. These people were not serving my God, and it seemed they were getting away with murder! I wanted what was due to me. In my arrogance I told God, "I serve you, yet you bless them instead of me." I just did not understand why.

An entire year of my life was spent trying to be a **good** Christian, yet all I did was wait and wait. Well, my days of waiting were over. I was going to take what was rightfully mine. So I joined the world and partook of their sins in search of what I thought was happiness.

Of my own free will I made a conscious decision to return to the world. Do not let anyone convince you that going back into the world will be an overnight process. I have heard it said that our actions do not just change in one day; it takes time. For me, it would take just a year of my life and I would be back in the world.

The first thing I did after making the decision to return to my vomit was to shorten my attendance at church. Secondly, I stopped praying. Within a matter of time, my prayer life was completely gone. I did not even bother to say grace anymore. My heart was becoming bitter as each day passed, but there were still things in the world that bothered me; things like injustice and the cry of the poor were always on my mind. Although I still had my Bible, I did not read it. It was right where I had left it, stuffed away on that same shelf collecting dust. My mind was set on finding my way back into the world, back to a world I once knew and loved. For one reason or another, I "felt" as if I was missing out on something in the world, and I had to find out what it was. So, as many Christians do, I returned to the very things God had delivered me from: *I* returned to the vomit.

- As a dog returneth to his vomit, so a fool returneth to his folly. — *Proverbs 26:11 (KJV)*

I had gotten to a point in my life where I could see distance growing between God and myself. It was getting harder and harder to feel his presence. Of course, the one thing the devil was sure to do was to isolate me from my Christian friends. I must admit it worked beautifully. After some time had passed, the Christians I had prayed with, witnessed with, and grew to love, no longer had anything in common with me. Had it not been for the prayers of a few dedicated Christians who knew what it meant to love someone in spite of their sins, my fall could have been detrimental. In my heart I knew I was headed down the wrong path. They cared so deeply for me that they simply refused to let me go.

During the opportunities when I did talk with Christians, their conversation always led back to God, a God I was struggling to forget. I guess it is safe to say that I was secretly angry with God. God had promised that he would supply all my needs, so where was my fancy car? Where was all the money he promised?

At that time, I was blind. I could not see all the other blessings God had already given me. I did not think about the roof over my head, or the food that he supplied for me daily, not to mention my health. Sometimes at night as I slept, I would often feel great conviction. In the morning when I rose, I would tell God I was sorry, only to ease my own selfish pain of shame and disgrace. After I prayed, I would end my prayer by telling him that I still loved him. But the second the words left my lips, I would go out committing sin after sin.

The Lord is merciful and even in our stupidity he does not change. Soon, he began to send labors across my path. It baffled me at the amount of Christians I was meeting. I met so many Christians that it was getting ridiculous; the majority of them did not even know my name! No matter how disinterested I seemed, they would minister to me anyway. The conviction of their words about God's love was convicting my spirit and bringing life back into my soul!

As the word of God says: "The devil comes immediately to steal the seeds that are sown into the hearts of a believer." While a Christian stood ministering to me, it was as if I could also hear Satan's lies crashing into my ears. I took my palms and pressed them against my ears as he fought to keep me from hearing the word of God. Although I thought I was alone, the Holy Spirit was also present, tugging at my heart to return to a Father who loved me. Thought after thought entered my mind and I could not stop thinking about God's love. I was in a spiritual war. Christians were praying for me to be free of the devil, while the devil was fighting to keep hold of the thoughts that entered my mind. All the while, I could not stop thinking about God's love while wishing the devil would remain silent. My spiritual man was too weak to fight. I had not fed him in over a year.

This beautiful God-fearing woman stood praying and dropping seeds of love into my soul. As I stood listening to her speak words of wisdom into my heart, the devil was still busy shooting arrows into my mind. As shameful as it sounds, my mind began to reflect back to a time when I was comparing my blessings to others. I knew in my heart that it was time to make yet another decision.

I was starting to remember again. I thought about all the material things I did not have, as well as all the sins I had committed before God. I felt there was no way out for me; I had gone too far and could not see how God could reach me. As I thought of these beautiful Christians, another seed of doubt was being planted in my mind. Yet it was time to make another decision. I had been in the world too long, so I gave ear to Satan as he talked about the Christians. I can still recall the lies he whispered in my ears. The biggest lie he told me was that I was unworthy of God's love, and all the Christians that talked to me, secretly looked down on me. I bought into the lie. There was just no way around it; the

Christians had to go! No matter what it took, in my mind I was convinced that I had to avoid Christians at all cost. As I reflect back on my past, I thank God for those Christians who did not carry their feelings on their shoulders. They walked in love and in the spirit. They could see beneath the mask. I was lost and needed them more than I realized. My insults did not shake them, and trying to offend a Christian who is grounded in God's word is not an easy thing to do. My cruel words rolled off their backs—water on the back of a duck. I was simply amazed by their love, and whether I would admit it or not, their love was affecting me.

Being so unkind to a Christian is not easy because they are so kind. No matter how rude I was, they returned nothing to me but love. To say the least, they were killing the hate and the unforgiveness inside of me. They were killing my hate with their love. These people had committed no crime. They were doing what Jesus had told them to do: Keep his Commandments by loving the Lord God with all their heart, with all their might and all their soul. And loving their neighbor as they love themselves.

- And thou shalt love the LORD thy God with all thine heart, and with all thy soul, and with all thy might. — *Deuteronomy 6:5 (KJV)*

- Thou shalt not avenge, nor bear any grudge against the children of thy people, but *thou shalt love thy neighbour as thyself*: I am the LORD. — *Leviticus 19:18 (KJV)*

- Master, which is the great commandment in the law?

14

- Jesus said unto him, *Thou shalt love the Lord thy God with all thy heart, and with all thy soul, and with all thy mind.*

- This is the first and great commandment.

- And the second is like unto it, *Thou shalt love thy neighbour as thyself.*

- On these two commandments hang all the law and the prophets. — *Matthew 22:36-40 (KJV)*

Letter Three
Workers in the Vineyard

Years were passing. I was still walking in darkness. The blinders were still on my eyes. At times, tiny specks of sunlight did find its way around the patches on my eyes, but I saw more darkness than light.

I found acceptance amongst my worldly friends. They played a vital role in helping me to forget the church. All their cruel jokes and harsh comments about Christians gave me the confidence I needed to enjoy my sinful life. It *sounds* better to say that I hated being with them and sinning, but that is a lie. Sin felt good to me while I was doing it. I later realized that I enjoyed being with my worldly friends because there were no rules. We could say whatever we wanted, and no matter how much we sinned, we could always laugh about it later. I was laughing on the outside, but on the inside my heart was breaking. Although I was working hard on putting the church behind me, I could still feel the Holy Spirit tugging at my heart to return to my Lord.

When a Christian falls, God will always come back to get you. He will not just give up on you. He still had not given up on me. Within a matter of time, days had turned into weeks, and the weeks into months. In the end, I was back in the world for six years. Soon something miraculous would happen in my life, something so miraculous and real that it would open my eyes and redirect my focus back on God.

In November of 2008, one of my best friends died from a heart attack. James was my first love. I had loved

16

him since I was a teenager. I had been loving him for so long that when he died I felt like a part of me had died also. James taught me how to dance, and it was him whom I chose to sin with. We both walked in darkness hand in hand, as we encouraged each other and kept the truth hidden about the things we did in the dark.

One day while out celebrating, I called James. We both joked about living the good life. James and I got a kick out of rubbing each other's noses in things. All of our jokes always ended with a strong belly laugh. The call I would make on that day did not leave me laughing. The day I received the news is as clear in my mind as if it happened yesterday. I stood amongst a restaurant filled with entrepreneurs. My company had been chosen to dine in a fancy restaurant and I also received the pleasure of riding in a stretch limousine, all at their expense. I could not wait to call James and tell him where I was and how much I was loving the moment. I picked up my cell phone and stepped outside so I could hear him better and talk a little trash. The telephone rang three times when suddenly a man answered the phone. I immediately asked to speak to James.

"He is no longer here," the man responded.

I frowned as I drew my lips inside my mouth. "Oh, did he leave for the day?" I asked.

The man paused. "No ma'am, he's gone."

I ran my fingertips across my forehead and exhaled. "What do you mean he's gone? Are you saying he's left work for the day or has he stepped away from his desk?"

The man's voice came blaring through the phone like I was stuck on stupid. He uttered the words I never

17

thought I would hear. "He's dead! They had his funeral a week ago!"

I flipped my phone closed while his voice echoed in my ears. As I rested my back against the brick wall of the restaurant, I tried to hold back my tears. My emotions were turning inside of me like a tornado. *How could this be?* I wondered. Later on, I got the full story from a member of his family. James had awakened and stepped out of bed preparing for his day, when suddenly his body fell limp onto the floor. As he clutched his chest gasping for his last breath, my best friend lay dying and no one was there who could save him.

After hearing about James's death, I remember driving down the road on a rainy night and I could no longer see the road before me. I pulled over and released my seat belt and rested my head on the passenger seat, and curled up and cried like a child. His death was a reality check.

Anger was the first emotion I experienced. In my mind, I felt that his death was my punishment for turning away from the Lord. *God is paying me back*, I thought. I told God as I lay in the front seat of my car, "If you really wanted to hurt me, you did!" As I cried what seemed like rivers of tears, I could not get my best friend's face out of my mind. Like others who had lost a loved one, I later found the strength to rise to my feet and go on with my life.

God is so merciful and loving, that during my fall he did not take back the gifts he had given me. I found it odd that even though I had returned to the world, the talents God gave me were still operating within me. My discernment was not as strong as it once was, but I still had discernment. I still remembered God's word, and I still knew how to pray, although I refused to, especially after James died.

Death had not left my life. Two years prior to James's death, I had lost another friend named Lisa. Lisa was like my sister. She was a true friend who helped me deal with a lot of hurt that stemmed from my childhood. She was also someone I both loved and trusted; she would be the one person to keep all my secrets. We went to party after party and were there for each other when necessary. She would bring much joy into my life before the day she would leave me forever. One day I got a strange phone call from Lisa. She had called to tell me good-bye, although I did not realize it until three hours later that she was saying good-bye forever. She explained how much she loved me, and reminded me that no one is here to stay. I was confused, but I clung to the receiver. Lisa continued to tell me just how much I had affected her life, and how much she cared. If I only knew that my friend was calling to say good-bye, I would have kept her on the phone a lot longer. Later that evening, around six o'clock, I received a phone call from a fellow co-worker. Lisa had suffered a heart attack in the bathroom and died earlier that day at work. I screamed into the receiver as my heart split down the middle. "Why God, why?"

After Lisa's death, James helped me get through it. I spent many nights on the phone crying to him about losing her, not realizing that within the next two years I would lose him as well. The two friends I loved more than any other were gone. There I was, left alone with no one I could trust. They were my best friends, but the reality was that they were both gone. However, the good news about Lisa is that she had accepted Jesus as her savior before she died. But as for James, his path would be different.

James's death was a wakeup call for me. I felt like the walking dead—numb. The two friends I loved most were taken away from me, and I was left feeling so empty.

A couple of weeks passed when I surprisingly ran into a godly woman who had been praying for me. The moment her eyes met mine, I knew exactly what she was thinking. The expression on her face spoke loud and clear. As she spoke, often I would drop my eyes looking everywhere except into hers. All I could feel was shame for the sinning I was doing. I also blamed myself for both of my friends' deaths. If I had only been walking in the light and following the Lord, maybe he would have spared them. I tormented myself every time I thought about James. I told myself I could have said something to him about Jesus, I could have done more for him. I was a sinner just as filthy as the rest of the world.

After reading the book of Romans my eyes began to open.

- For all have sinned, and come short of the glory of God. — *Romans 3:23 (KJV)*

- Now we know that what things soever the law saith, it saith to them who are under the law: that every mouth may be stopped, and all the world may become guilty before God. — *Romans 3:19 (KJV)*

What could this woman possibly say to me to ease the hurt in my heart? When I did finally look into her eyes, all I could see was love. Her presence was like standing in a whirlwind of love and being pulled inside of it.

- For by grace are ye saved through faith; and that not of yourselves: it is the gift of God:

- Not of works, lest any man should boast.
  — *Ephesians 2:8-9 (KJV)*

I was a backslider saved by grace. During that time in my life I did not feel worthy of God's love or forgiveness because I had not been very good, nor had I done anything to earn my salvation. Thank God for his grace.

Finally, the woman invited me to church, and then told me she had been praying for me. This was a bold woman of God, she meant what she said, and she said exactly what she meant. She began by telling me the story about the man who had some sheep.

What do you think? If a man owned a hundred sheep, and one of them wanders away, will he not leave the ninety-nine on a hill and go to look for the one that wanders off? And if he finds it, I tell you the truth, he is happier about that one sheep than about the ninety-nine that did not wander off. In the same way your Father in heaven is not willing that any of these little ones should be lost. — *Matthew 18:12-14 (KJV)*

As she told me the parable, her words were like fire burning inside my ears. No matter how I tried to change the subject, her mind stayed fixed on the story. Finally, I had heard enough. I folded my arms across my chest and exhaled hard as I pressed my lips together. I stood searching for an excuse to leave. Without warning, she caught me completely off guard and wrapped her arms around me, and whispered in my ear, "Jesus loves you and there is nothing that can separate you from his love. God knows your heart," she explained. "And he knows it is good and that you are broken. But God has a plan for you. He is not finished with you yet." Still clinging to each of my shoulders, she looked me in the eyes and softly asked, "Why don't you come to church with me sometimes? We would sure love to have you."

Go to church? I thought. *There is no way that's going to happen.* I stood speechless. I did not want to hurt her feelings because she was so kind, but in my mind, I felt I was just too far gone for anybody to save me, even God. She stood patiently waiting for my answer as I again looked away from her. "No, I can't. I've been kind of busy. Besides, I haven't been to church in years."

"It's okay, God." She smiled. "The Lord will not hold your past against you. He will accept you just as you are, if you only ask for his forgiveness . . ." As she spoke, I took a step back while she was still talking. Her words reminded me of how dirty I was, and then my flesh rose up strong against her.

I blurted out, "I don't go to church anymore. That life for me is over. Now please leave me alone. I don't want to offend you." Again, she took a step toward me and placed her hands on my shoulders. She glanced up at the sky as if she was waiting on God to tell her what to say to me.

"I respect your wishes," she said. "But I want to leave you with something to think about. While you are out sinning and doing things to satisfy your flesh, your soul should feel the conviction of the Holy Spirit. That feeling you get in your heart is a good thing. The Holy Spirit convicts you. The devil condemns you. It is a good thing when *things* bother you. That is how the Holy Spirit leads you back to God, through your heart. But on the day when things no longer bother you, you'll know on that day that you are in a very bad place.

"I want you to remember what I've said," she continued. "Because in case you did not know it, God does give people over to a reprobate mind. Believe me, you don't want that. Seek the Lord while there is still time because tomorrow is not promised." After she spoke her peace, she released her hold of me and said her final words. "God loves you, and I am going to be praying for you." After speaking all that was in her heart, she slowly turned and walked away.

During my drive home, I kept thinking about her. Her words had upset me. Now I was mad! *Who gave her the right to talk to me like that?* I fussed and fussed as I drove my car over the speed limit. I cut in and out of lanes just trying to get home as I kept thinking about what this woman had said. *And who exactly does she think she is?* However, the woman's powerful words had touched my heart.

When I arrived home, I walked through my entire apartment and closed all the blinds. I sat in my dim living room in complete silence as her words ran around and around in my head. Although I was alone, I could still hear the impact of her words. Like so many times before, I pressed my palms against both my ears to drown out the sound of her voice. Her words were words of truth and power and they had cut me deep.

- For the word of God is quick, and powerful, and sharper than any two-edged sword, piercing even to the dividing asunder of soul and spirit, and of the joints and marrow, and is a discerner of the thoughts and intents of the heart. — *Hebrews 4:12 (KJV)*

I could not prove it, but I knew God had sent that woman across my path. Like other times, I pushed thoughts of returning to him out of my mind, and became preoccupied with other things. Although her words offended me, I could not stop thinking about her. There was one word in particular she used that bothered me the most, and that was the word "reprobate." *What did she mean by calling me reprobate?* In as much as I did not want to read the Bible, I searched for that word and this is what it said:

- And even as they did not like to retain God in *their* knowledge, God gave them over to **a reprobate mind**, to do those things which are not convenient;

- Being filled with all unrighteousness, fornication, wickedness, covetousness, maliciousness; full of envy, murder, debate, malignity; whisperers,

- Backbiters, haters of God, despiteful, proud, boasters, inventors of evil things, disobedient to parents,

24

- Without understanding, covenant breakers, without natural affection, implacable, unmerciful:

- Who knowing the judgment of God, that they which commit such things are worthy of death, not only do the same, but have pleasure in them that do them. — *Romans 1:28-32 (KJV)*

Worthy of death! I do not mind telling you that reading those scriptures scared me. I started going down the list to see how close I was to becoming a reprobate. Whew! I still had a long way to go before that happened to me. I assumed by the list that by the time someone became reprobate, God had finally accepted the fact that a person's soul would be lost forever. I must admit my fear of becoming a reprobate frightened me. My eyes were again beginning to open a bit more. I re-read the scripture again, not realizing that I was dropping seeds into my own heart.

Wow! Just think, people get *pleasure* in seeing other people doing the same wrong things that they are doing. After I learned what reprobate meant, I was determined not to become a reprobate. No matter what I did, I was not going down that road.

I did not understand my own state of mind at the time. I had not realized it, but God knew as each day passed that I was becoming blind. Only he could open my eyes to see the truth. Satan had fed me so many lies, lies that I had digested well. In my past, God had promised not to forsake me.

Before I fell, I honestly prayed and asked him that if I should ever get lost, to please come and find me. I have heard people say that they, "Have found the Lord!" The truth of the matter is that God does not get lost, we do! This was the prayer I prayed even when things were going well in my life. The last thing I wanted to do was to become blind to the truth, but God is faithful and he did not forget his promises.

- And I will bring the blind by a way that they knew not; I will lead them in paths that they have not known: I will make darkness light before them, and crooked things straight. These things will I do unto them, and not forsake them. — *Isaiah 42:16 (KJV)*

Letter Four
Knock! Knock! Who's There?

Years and years were passing, ten to be exact and I was still falling deeper into the world. I rarely ever thought about church anymore. I was continuing in disobedience by not listening to God, but he was determined not to give up on me.

The Christians were not the only way God tried to communicate with me; he began to give me spiritual dreams. He was sending me messages from all directions, but I still would not hearken to his voice. Don't ask me why I was being so rebellious, because I don't even know myself. I admit that I was conscious of the sin in my life, and yes, as awful as it sounds, I also realized I was doing a terrible thing by turning my back on God.

In my past, my only desire was to know and please God, yet I stood by and practically threw him away. But there was something inside of me pulling at me to stay in the world. I wrestled daily with an invisible enemy, an enemy who was clinging to my body and refusing to let go. I must give praise to God. The Lord still had my soul and he was taking claim of it! I would wrestle with that invisible enemy every day until God would utter the word, "Enough!"

- For we wrestle not against flesh and blood, but against principalities, against powers, against the rulers of the darkness of this world, against spiritual wickedness in high places.
— *Ephesians 6:12 (KJV)*

27

Have you ever had a desire for a certain food that you really love? After some time passes you still have the desire for that food, but you still have not tasted it. Your mind reflects back on how good it tasted, and how nice it would be to have just one more bite. That was when my heart began to yearn for God.

One day I saw a lady standing on a corner passing out some small books to anyone who would take one. After walking for what seemed like miles down a street filled with people, my feet led me to her. "Jesus loves you," she told the people passing by. From a few feet away I stood looking at the glow in her eyes as she smiled at the world. Not one person stopped to receive a single book from her hand. In my heart, I began to feel bad considering everyone was ignoring her, so I stepped forward. Without uttering a word she placed a small book in my hand and continued to extend her hand out to the people who passed by. As I walked away from her, I glanced at the small book. It read, *The Daily Bread*. I clung tight to the little book as I walked away. Before I crossed the busy street, I looked back at the woman and marveled. In my heart, I envied her because she was doing something wonderful. She was standing up and telling the whole world about God.

When I reached home, I rested the book on my coffee table where it lay for many days. Each morning as I reached for the remote to turn on the television I would glance at the book often, but not once picking it up. Then one morning I got up as I had many times before, but that day would be different. Instead of reaching for the remote, I stared at the little book. It was like a magnet drawing me to it. No longer could I resist the small book. I leaned forward, picked it up and popped open a soda and began to read.

Reading the words in that book was like medicine to a wounded heart. It was like the best milkshake I had ever had, or the best burger I have ever tasted. I must admit it felt good reading God's word again. I was turning page after page filling the very depths of my soul with each word. The words were like medicine to my soul. Without realizing the time, I had sat and read the entire book.

After I completed the book, I leaned back in my easy chair and stared up at the ceiling. I sat reliving moments spent with God as my mind flashed back to the time before my fall. I smiled inside as I thought of how I used to fall to my knees and pray every morning when I awakened. I would always fall to my knees and thank God for another day. That is how dedicated I was to God during those days. He was everything to me and his word was my pride and joy! Knowing him made me feel so alive and I was proud to be called *his child*.

That small book with such powerful words reminded me how much I had missed spending time with the Lord and reading the Bible. How could I have forgotten the beautiful songs of praise that I used to hear every Sunday as the choir sang? Hearing Christians singing in the church brought so much peace to my soul. All things were coming back to my remembrance. I even remembered how I used to keep my television tuned in to Christian networks. I used to get so excited hearing the different ministers talk about the Lord.

The *word* alone was exciting, but like everything else in my life, too much had changed. I had changed the channels. My new favorite channels had become talk shows and sitcoms. Do not get me wrong, there is nothing wrong with watching movies and listening to some of the world's most beautiful love songs, but my problem was discretion. I would watch and listen to anything. The only requirement was that it made me feel good. Sometimes I would listen to secular music and watch R-rated movies all night.

It was true, I had become worldly, so worldly that I was convinced that there was no way I could ever find my way back into God's arms again. The devil had me convinced that God hated me. I believed him, too, because I hated myself. How could God love me in spite of all the sinning I had done in my life? On that day, I sat down and wrote God a poem. The poem was called: *The Monster Inside of Me*. This is the poem I wrote to the Lord and still have today:

Dear God,

I have traveled all around the world in search of love, so desperate to have it, I gave everything up. I had lover after lover trying to find someone to fill the void inside. Dear Lord, please help me find my way back to you, before I lose the rest of my mind.

You blessed me to accomplish a lot in my life. And with tears in my eyes I always remembered that it was only you. But because of the softness of my heart, I have been used a time or two, always quick to give up anything, yet again waiting to be used.

Lord, I stand against the world as the cold wind blows against my face, with a large chip growing on my shoulder, as my hearts grows colder and colder.

I don't want to live this life while living a lie in a world that I despise. No one can understand how I feel. When darkness comes, I find my escape in a bottle of pills. Only in my dreams can I find any real peace. Dear God, can you really love me in spite of this monster inside of me?

During my high school days, I thought the friends I had would last forever, not realizing that life changes people like it changes the weather. Some of my friends got lost along the way, choosing the wrong path, leading to an early grave. I had to learn a simple fact: everybody is not going to love me, some people take their love back.

I've lived most of my life in the spotlight. My passion for creating never seemed to die. I've written poetry, love songs, and even a novel, as the world clicked on the face on the web, and read about me the author.

When I stand before the public, people look at me wishing they had my life. They want to be a writer and a published author. They have seen my face on the front pages and heard my sultry voice over the radio waves, I feel the piercing look in their eyes as they sit and stare as they wish for all that is mine.

On my last day on earth, I hope someone will remember me and know the truth, so that I will finally be free. I hope when I am gone someone will stand up and say, she loved from her heart in a very special way. But most of all, God, I pray that you will give me what I long for when I ask you on my last day on earth, to please open heaven's door.

Lord, I don't want to live this life while living a lie in a world that I despise. No one understands how I really feel. When darkness comes, I find my escape in a bottle of pills. Only in my dreams can I find any real peace. Dear God, can you still love me in spite of this monster inside of me?

I hated myself during that time in my life. There was a monster living inside of me, a monster I could not control, and this thing was destroying my life. I didn't want to live, but I didn't want to die either.

There was a big void in my life, an emptiness inside of me that longed to be filled. As I sat and thought of the wreck I had made of my life, godly sorrow began to fill my heart as the tears began to flow. I felt so ashamed of what I had been doing. I knew of the terrible fate that awaited me. And what about God? What was I going to say to him on the day I met him face to face? I had to at least try to get him to understand why I did all the terrible things I did. I told myself that even if he didn't forgive me, at least I would have told him the truth. I owed him that much. So I dropped to my knees and begin to pray, when suddenly the memory of every sin I had ever committed attacked my mind!

Letter Five
But You Gotta Have Friends!

There were things I had forgotten about, but they were coming back. I was beginning to remember them as clear as day. All I could hear was backlash and unworthiness. The voice was so ingrained in my heart I had to stop praying. I rose to my feet and wiped away my tears. Who was I kidding? I had gone too far. The love affairs I had in my past were enough by themselves to cause God to throw me in the Lake of Fire! I turned and headed for the bathroom as I wiped the tears from my eyes.

While standing over the bathroom sink, I turned on the faucet and let the water run. I reached for the soap, lathered up the towel, and began washing my face. After my face was clean, I searched for a towel to dry off the remaining beads of water. Slowly, I stood erect looking at the reflection of the person I had become. Were my eyes deceiving me? I stepped closer to the mirror and began to touch my face. Glancing into the mirror was like looking into the eyes of a stranger. The towel dropped to the floor as I continued to stare at my likeness. Again, I caressed the side of my face as I leaned closer to the mirror turning my face from side to side.

Something was changing. I had been washing my face every day, but at that moment I saw something that disturbed me. I told myself it must have been the soap. Again, I washed my face a second time. This time I would use a different kind of soap. After the second washing, nothing changed. My skin looked dark and dull, almost dirty. I washed my face vigorously, scrubbing and scrubbing, making sure I had gotten rid of any film or residue. With my eyes remaining closed, I felt for the towel and then began to dry my skin. When I opened my eyes, I was hoping I would see the old reflection of myself that I had seen in the past, but much to my surprise nothing had changed.

Dear God! My countenance was changing. Where was the light that separated me from the sinners? I must have washed my face that day until my skin felt raw, but still no change. *What was happening to me?* I wondered. I sat on the bare floor of my bathroom with my back resting against the cabinet as the sound of running water still rang loud in my ears. I felt lost and confused as I pondered the reflection of the person I had become. Again, thought after thought ran through my mind, when suddenly the sound of a ringing telephone interrupted my illusion of the past. I pulled myself up from the floor and rose to my feet. When I reached the phone, I lifted the receiver, but did not say a word. Suddenly a familiar voice came into my ears.

"Hello? Hello?" said the caller. Immediately I recognized the voice. It was my friend, Monique. She was calling to see what my plans were for the night.

I had met Monique in New York one night while in a club. She was seated at the bar and downing one drink after another. I stood trying to get the bartender's attention, but he just kept walking past as if I were invisible. Finally, Monique asked if I needed the bartender.

"That would be nice," I replied.

In the snap of a finger, Benny the bartender came to Monique as if she were somebody famous. He then turned his attention to me. "What are you having?" he asked, leaning over the counter and polishing a glass.

"I'll have a beer," I responded.

Monique quickly turned her head and looked at me as if I had insulted the man. "You have got to be kidding!" She laughed as she took a sip of her fancy drink.

"No, I'd really like a beer," I said.

Monique looked towards Benny and smirked as she ordered for me. "Benny, give her an apple martini," she insisted. I had never had an apple martini before. I was just hoping it did not cost much, because all I had was seven bucks in my pocket. When Benny returned, he sat my drink on the counter. I slid my hand inside my pocket in search of my last seven dollars, but Monique insisted I put my money away. We ended up sitting on our bar stools and talking until closing. If alcohol is truly a truth serum, Monique must have drank a gallon, because she sat pouring her heart out to me as if she had known me all of her life. Benny kept her glass filled each time she emptied it as I sat listening to her talk about her father, her mother, and her miserable life. That is when I realized who Monique was—the poor little rich girl I had heard about all my life.

From that night on, she had taken me under her wing. Whenever we went out, she always introduced me as her best friend. There were times when I questioned how anyone so rich could be so unhappy? Monique was everything I wanted to be. She had popularity, a beautiful home that looked like a mansion, and if that was not enough, she was beautiful as well. Monique was also the first white woman I had ever "hung out" with. She would often say how much she envied my cocoa brown skin. Oftentimes she would say how much she hated the winter because she would always lose her beautiful tan.

Everybody loved Monique or so it seemed. The party didn't begin until she showed up. Being her best friend made me somebody. I had finally become part of the "in crowd," which was very important to me at that time. I was calling important people by their first names. It was nothing for her to order the best champagne and take me along with her to expensive restaurants.

Our friendship lasted off and on for about two years. There were times when she would disappear for months, and then without warning, she would show up at my door high as usual. We would sit in the kitchen and get high together as we talked about old times.

When I was a child, I suffered from low self-esteem and rejection. Having a friend like Monique made me feel important. She was living the life I had dreamed of living. Because of her, I was meeting influential people, eating in nice restaurants, and living the good life. After years of waiting and waiting, I was finally hanging out with the "Joneses."

Having money and being able to eat in upscale restaurants was nice. One day she surprised me and took me on a shopping spree. Afterwards, she gave me five-hundred dollars for nothing. All the things she was doing for me would come with a price, but I had no idea how great the price would be.

Again, it was time to shop. Monique would say, "You need some new clothes. I cannot have someone hanging out with me who dresses like a homeless person." So she bought me more clothes. I thought my clothes were nice. They did not have any designer labels on them, but they were clean.

There is nothing wrong with wanting nice things, but I guess both of our motives were wrong. It wasn't until later that I realized Monique had bought me just like she bought her designer shoes. I was no more than a toy to drag around town with her. At her command I was ready to go wherever she wanted to go. My conscience was kicking me in my rear, hard.

My life then revolved around pleasing a woman who did not have a heart for God. The only thing Monique cared about was having fun and spending money, and that was fine with me, because I had grown tired of taking pop bottles back to the store for some extra change.

My new family of friends consisted of people who had no idea of God's love, and couldn't care less about his word. People like Monique only believed in what they could see, and what they could feel, and that was money! The moment I hung up the receiver, a scripture came into my heart.

- Fret not thyself because of evildoers, neither be thou envious against the workers of iniquity.

- For they shall soon be cut down like the grass, and wither as the green herb.

- Trust in the Lord, and do good; so shalt thou dwell in the land, and verily thou shalt be fed.
  — *Psalm 37:1-3 (KJV)*

My question for God was: When was I going to be fed? When were the evildoers going to be cut down? It seemed to me once again that they were prospering. Besides, I thought it was too late for me. I acknowledged my sins before God and was ready to accept my punishment. I did not have time anymore—no time for the church, no time for the Christians and especially no time for the preacher man.

I had friends now, friends with money. As cold as it sounds, I just did not have time to wait anymore. I was tired of waiting and that's just the way it was.

Letter Six
Everything Comes Out in the Rinse

I resumed my call with Monique that day. I wondered what she had in mind for the night. After the meltdown I had in the bathroom, I needed to go. Although I tried to clear my throat so she could not hear that I had been crying, she could sense that something was wrong.

"You sound weird," she remarked. "Are you okay?"

"Yes," I lied as I tried to take in all that I had just experienced. "Monique, everything is fine," I said convincingly. "Please stop acting like a mother hen."

"Hey, let's go out tonight. I feel like clubbing!" she insisted.

"Oh, I don't know," I quickly answered as I ran my hand against my face.

"Awww, come on! I won't take no for an answer. Get yourself together. I'll be there to pick you up around ten." Before I could say another word, Monique hung up the phone. I knew what she would do if I refused to go. She was the nuttiest white woman I had ever met. I knew she would drive up and blast her horn until I came outside. So to avoid any embarrassment from my neighbors, once she arrived I stepped out of my door and into her car. She burned rubber while pulling away from the curb.

Whatever Monique wanted she always got. *Maybe she is right about me going out tonight*, I thought. After all, I did need a drink, and a strong one. After what I had gone through earlier, I needed a whole bottle. When we reached the club, we sat in her car and did our usual routine of getting high and drinking before we went in. I was so high I felt like I could touch the sky. Monique was not far behind, although I think she had sniffed a little too much of that white powder.

Once we stepped inside the club, it was simply amazing the effect Monique had on men. They carried on like sick puppies each time they saw her. It was the craziest thing I had ever seen! They loved Monique. She was their queen, and was so popular she never paid to get in any club. The bouncers who worked the doors also had huge crushes on Monique and always let her in without question. Men loved her. I would just sit back and watch the show as they fought for her attention. I was already high as a kite, and watching Monique in action really amplified my high on an even higher level.

If anybody could lift my spirits, Monique could. One night we drank so many shots of tequila that I had to quit. I knew if I had one more shot I was going down for the count. The crowd in the club was growing smaller as we both sat in our booth and swore to party until dawn. The DJ changed songs and began to play one of Monique's favorite songs. She reached out and pulled me by the arm, leading me to the dance floor. I was a bit uncomfortable, but I did not complain; I simply followed her lead. We stood on the dance floor shaking our hips until they could no longer rattle. After a few songs, we both grew tired of dancing and returned to the booth. As usual, Monique called for more drinks.

"That's it for me," I insisted as I waved my hand. "If I drink another glass of anything, I'm going to pass out right here on this table." We both laughed heartily, but she ordered herself a drink anyway.

It was obvious Monique could not hold her liquor very well, but she always seemed to be in control of everything, even me. I used to wonder if she knew how lucky she was to be able to buy whatever she wanted, but I never asked. But in her eyes I could see that she was unhappy. It was all just a show. After spending as much time as we spent together, after a while you get to know a person pretty well. The booze opened her heart, and out of it came many confession, confessions that I was not sure I needed to know.

"Did you know my father owns the biggest car dealership in the state?" she asked.

"No, I didn't. That's cool," I added.

"Cool? That son of a gun cares more about those stupid cars than he cares about me!"

I could see the tears filling up in her eyes, but instead of allowing them to fall she swallowed them.

"And my *so-called* mother isn't any better," she added. "She spends half of her life traveling around the world shopping for things she does not need."

Well that explained all the fancy cars Monique was driving. She had money, but she did not have anyone to show her real love, especially not her parents. I think as I reflect back on my past, that is what drew me to her. Like me, she was brokenhearted. I had a way of making people feel good even when they were sad. I took pride in being a good listener. I realized as we sat drinking our eyeballs out, that in her heart she wanted more than just money from her parents, she wanted their love.

The thought of love reminded me of my reflection I had seen earlier that day. I began rubbing my face again. Monique kept asking what was wrong.

"What's up with you tonight?" she asked as she sipped from her glass of wine. "Why do you keep rubbing your face? Do you have some kind of skin disease or something?" I pulled out a cigarette, lit it and took a long draw on it.

"I'm fine, Monique. Can we just drop it?"

"Drop what? You still haven't told me what's wrong, and I'm not going to shut up about it until you do. So what's up?" she demanded as she slammed her glass down against the table. It became quite clear to me that Monique was not going to let up. I knew if I didn't tell her something, she would bug me all night until I did. "So, what is it?" she asked again as she rested her elbows on the table and leaned toward me.

I cleared my throat and took another puff of my cigarette. "Monique, I know you. If I told you, you'd just laugh."

"Aww, come on!" she demanded. "For crying out loud, I won't laugh. Scouts honor," she promised, signaling the oath with her two fingers. "Talk to me, tell me what's wrong?"

Reluctantly, I lowered my guard. I leaned towards her and looked into her eyes. "Monique, take a real good look at my face," I said.

"Okay, what am I looking for?" she asked, squinting her eyes.

"Tell me, do I look any different to you? I mean, am I glowing?"

"Glowing? What are you talking about?" She laughed. "What did you do? Swallow a light bulb or something?"

"No, I didn't swallow a light bulb. What I mean is . . . well, you see . . . I have never told you this before, but I used to go to church a lot, but that was a long time ago. After I got saved I had this glow about me, but today when I looked in the mirror I noticed that I wasn't glowing anymore. I think I've lost something that I may never get back. Monique, please tell me the truth. When you look at me, can you tell that I am a Christian?" I sat quietly hoping she was going to say something sweet to ease my breaking heart. Instead of easing my mind, and bringing some peace into my heart, it felt like she picked up a sledgehammer and crushed me with it.

"Let me get this straight," she asked, resting her back against the booth we shared. "You want to know if I think you are a Christian? Is that about right?"

I covered my mouth and nodded a slow yes.

Monique leaned towards me again and spoke in a quiet tone. "Oookay, I'll just say this, if Christians do drugs outside in other people's cars, go clubbing and drink until they pass out, then yes, I think you are a Christian. If only in my dreams, you are definitely a Christian." She smirked.

"Monique, I'm serious! I really need to know what you think!" Monique thumped her empty glass on the table and looked me square in the eyes.

"Girlfriend, if you're a Christian, I'm a virgin!"

"What!" I was outraged to say the least! *How could she say such an awful thing to me?* So I got deep in the flesh and returned insult for insult. She had gone too far.

"You know what, Monique? You can go to hell!" I snapped. Now it was time to play the dozens. Monique was good at that. She came back with a quick response. She was always good at comebacks, and I had forgotten that.

"That's fine with me." She laughed. "At least when we get there we'll have each other. The Christian and the virgin!" She cackled. "Hey, you know what?" she continued as she puffed on the nearly gone out cigarette burning in the ashtray. "We should start a group. You know that I know everybody. Hey, I bet we could get a record deal!"

It was obvious Monique was making a joke out of my pain. I sat staring and regretting the day we'd ever met. *How could she be so cruel? What had I done to deserve that?* And just when I thought she was finished with her dramatics, she went even further. Monique staggered to her feet and called for the attention of everybody in the bar. "Hey everybody. Listen up! Listen up! I have an announcement to make."

Benny walked towards the CD player. He did exactly as Monique requested and turned the music completely down as he and everyone within earshot waited for Monique to speak.

"Tonight in our midst we have two celebrities," she explained. "That's right! There is me of course, yours truly, the virgin." She spoke loudly as all the people in the bar began to laugh. "And believe it or not, we also have right here before our very eyes, a full breathing Christian right here!" She pointed as every eye fell on me. "So here is the question I want to ask tonight. Is there anybody here tonight in need of our services?"

Some man yelled, "Hell yeah! You girls can come home with me. My wife is out of town, but I doubt if she would mind me having a little company, considering your friend is a Christian and all. Hell, I might even get a few of them devils to leave my house if she showed up!" After his comment, everybody started laughing. I was so embarrassed and had no idea how to respond to his remark. I only sat wishing I could have made myself invisible.

They were mocking me—making fun of me and for what? What had I done to deserve that? I felt like somebody had played a bad joke on me, and I was the butt of everybody's laughter. My eyes remained fixed on Monique as she stood laughing so hard that she could no longer stand. Without breaking my stare, I rose to my feet. With my eyes locked on hers I said, "You are the biggest jerk I have ever met, and I hope to God I never see your face for the rest of my life!" I then turned and walked towards the door as the people sat staring and laughing at the comment made by the drunk who sat at the bar.

Monique had broken my heart. How could she do that? What had I done to her? I thought to myself: *She wasn't making fun of me, she was mocking God, that's what she was doing.* That night was the end of our friendship as far as I was concerned. The alcohol was no excuse for her behavior. I did not care about them attacking me, but they were practically mocking God! I told myself that they were nothing but a bar full of dirty sinners, and they were going to get exactly what they deserved!

It was a cold November night and I was mad, but as mad as I was at the time, I could not feel the cold wind against my skin. All I kept thinking about was how badly Monique had treated me. Her words were cruel and insensitive. How could she say such cruel things to me? She knew I was a Christian, although I never said it, but in my heart, I thought she knew I loved Jesus. I justified Monique's action in my mind. I assumed she acted cruel towards me because she was trying to hurt me for loving God. Then suddenly like a thunderbolt that had fallen from the sky, it hit me: "If you love Jesus so much then why are you following her instead of him?"

I did not have an answer, but the truth was there right in front of me. I had a long walk to make before I would reach my apartment, and a lot of time to think about the question that filled my mind. Because I had grown accustomed to Monique paying for everything, I did not even have money for a cab. So, if I was to reach my place, I would have to walk. I was very angry because my place was miles away, and it was very cold. I learned a hard lesson that night, a lesson I would never forget! The Bible says, "And we know that all things work together for good to them that love God, to them who are the called according to his purpose." Monique had tried to hurt me with her words, but all she did was drive me back into God's loving arms.

Letter Seven
The Prodigal Son

I returned to Detroit and tried to build my life there. In my heart, I longed for my true dream of becoming a great writer and director. I did not remain in Michigan for a year. I had to chase the dream I was dreaming.

In 1995, I packed my bags and headed back to New York. I was afraid, but I began something that I had not finished. My heart yearned to see my dreams come true. There are many roads we travel in life, yet not realizing how hard and long the road can be. I wanted that dream so bad I could taste it, but instead of reaching my dream, I failed and ended up living in a shelter. Day after day, I walked the streets of Manhattan, lost with nowhere to go. In my pocket I had two tokens for the subway, which I had received from the welfare office. Each day the people who ran the shelter would wake everybody up insisting we leave. By nightfall, we had to be back at the shelter before ten. At ten o'clock, the doors would be locked and if I did not make it back on time, I would have to spend the night sleeping in the street.

I was lost, trapped and knew I had really messed up. But through it all, God still had his hand on my life. I began talking to him again, asking him to help me find my way.

To get a fresh start on life, I enlisted in the United States Military. Maybe in the military I would find peace, or at least a sense of pride. I remained in the military for six years, regretting the day I had ever signed my name on the paper. They really do, do more by 9 A.M. than most people do all day. That was a warning not to enlist, but I signed my name on the contract anyway.

Throughout my military career I began to grow spiritually. As God still continued reaching out to me, he gave me the strength I needed to overcome, and the willingness to succeed. My soul began yearning for him every day. I was getting closer to true repentance, although I did not really see it.

After I got through basic training and graduated, I began to live my life as a soldier. I was proud to wear my uniform; to me it represented honor. Nevertheless, there was still something missing in my life. My first love was gone, and I was the one who had left him behind. It was time to pick up my cross and try again. I knew that I needed a church, so I went searching for a preacher man who would teach me the word of God.

One day while driving down the road, I passed a small church that sat near the base. I decided to go and visit on Sunday. When I arrived at the church, I found the members to be friendly. God did not tell me to go there, but I assumed it would be okay just as long as I was going to church, that was a step. I began to go every Sunday until a day came when I would no longer darken the doorway of that church ever again.

Unexpectedly, the pastor of the church made sexual advances towards me. He then lied and told me that God had told him that he had married the wrong woman, and I was to be his wife. That was another lesson the Lord taught me. You should not join a church just because the people seem friendly, and the preacher man knows how to get the members excited. You have to make sure the

Spirit of God is in control and the pastor is teaching from the word of God, The Holy Bible. The minister has to be a true servant of the Lord Jesus Christ. The Bible says you will know a tree by its fruit. The fruit on that pastor's tree were all rotten. I immediately became offended and walked away from the church. I knew God was not there, at least not the God that I knew.

After my military career ended, I did not go back to New York. I relocated to Michigan once again. I was fortunate to land a job with the Department of Corrections and very proud to wear the uniform. I had an important job that meant a lot to me. It was during that time that God stretched out his hand real heavy on my life.

Each day as I walked the grounds of the prison I would often think to myself how blessed I was to have my freedom, freedom to come and go as I pleased. Many people look down on prisoners. Some people treat them as if they are not human. But because my heart was truly changing, God was growing closer to me.

The years began to pass and God was blessing me with even more money. Money was the least of my worries. I was making more money in one pay check than most people were making all month.

Like Peter, storms came into my life and I again took my eyes off God. He had given me the power to profit, but I did not know how to handle it. After six years of walking those grounds, the spirit of the Lord was growing stronger in me. I began to hear the voice of the Holy Spirit inside of my heart. When I did sin, it bothered me and that was a good thing. I was still in connection with God.

A day came when the spirit of the Lord spoke to me and said, "The time has come for you to go from this place. Your work here is done and it is now time for you to do something new."

I said, "No God!" As a matter of fact I said to myself that it was Satan who was telling me to leave, but in my heart I knew it was the Holy Spirit, but my flesh did not want to give up the good money I was making, so I stayed, refusing to leave. The Holy Spirit would often speak through me to inmates and staff as the words came pouring out of my mouth: "I am not here to stay, I am only passing through." I would say this to anyone who would listen.

Although the Lord had given me many chances to go, I clung to my job, believing that I would always have a guaranteed paycheck with great benefits.

During my time working in the prison, God granted me the opportunity to witness to many of the prisoners, which I did despite the rules. God knew my heart. I had compassion for them, but not just for them, but also for people outside the bob wired fences. The inmates I was paid to watch and protect had made some bad choices, but who was I to condemn them? God loved those prisoners just as much he loved me. During the time when I worked as an officer, God opened my eyes to see them as he saw them.

I once heard somebody say: "You are going to be surprised by the people you see in heaven." As I think back on the days I wore the correctional officer uniform, it feels good knowing I had a chance to influence the inmates around me by the way I carried myself.

Every so often when people are put in positions of leadership, it can sometimes go to their head. I am grateful that God gave me a heart for people. He taught me how to love people, and allowed me to see them through his eyes. Unlike man, God looks on the heart. I realized that I was truly growing when I saw my willingness to forgive prisoners who had cursed me, or called me out of my name.

Oftentimes we forget that many of the apostles in the Old Testament were also imprisoned. You might say: "That was different." Well I have a revelation for you. Not everybody in prison is guilty. I used to tell prisoners despite what crime they had committed God still loved them.

There was also another thing God showed me while working as an officer. Did you know that some of God's people are in prison? That is their assignment to walk before the prisoners and be a testimony for Jesus. God has granted them favor with man because their heart is true to him.

I hope this book will find its way behind the walls of the prison. Because prisoners need to know that God loves them, too. The decision to serve him is not mine, but yours. You must make the choice to live for him. He has given us a promise that he will never leave us or forsake us. Remember, you can't pull the cover over your head and your feet at the same time with God. He sees everything. If you give your life to Jesus, he has promised that he will never leave or forsake you. Even now, God is opening the doors of the prison and allowing many to go free.

The choice is up to you. You can follow man, who has no hell or heaven to put you in or you can trust in God. As I stated earlier, during those time when I walked the prison grounds, God told me it was time for me to leave, but because of the money and the benefits, I stayed.

God gave me chance after chance to walk away, but I would not leave. Leaving my good paying job meant I would have to trust God to feed me, clothe me and provide for me. I was afraid to take that step. I was on top of the world. *Why risk what I had by leaving my good paying job?* I thought to myself.

Around that time pride had taken root in my heart because I had come so far. No longer was I a homeless woman who once slept on the street. At last, I was living the life! The Bible says: "God resists the proud." I wanted God in my life, but I wanted to decide when and how our relationship was going to work. To be honest, I needed to be in control. Although I wanted to, I did not know how to trust in something I could not see, but I was eager to learn. God knew I was sincere because he was looking at my heart.

Before God broke me down to my knees literally, each day I wore what I like to refer to as a mask. I carried myself very proud. There were times when I was actually becoming rather cocky. The mask I wore eluded the world so they could not see my tenderness and the softness of my heart. In the past, so many people had hurt me, that I built an invisible wall around myself. God allowed me to walk in my own dish of self-pride until he decided to break it. Anyone who knows me can tell you that during that time in my life, I thought I was God's finest creation.

You see, God had called me. He had been calling me for years, but I refused to answer. In my eyes, the life of a Christian seemed boring. I actually believed that all they did was pray and go to church seven days a week. I could not see myself living like a monk or a nun. I wanted to enjoy my life.

Later down the road, I would soon realize that I was not living at all. The only thing I was doing was merely existing. After I rededicated my life to the Lord, I realized that I had to change my friends. God said in his word that light and darkness cannot walk together. You cannot serve God and the devil at the same time. I had to make a choice, so I chose God. Yes, it is true, after I made my choice I lost some friends along the way because God said, "Come from amongst them and be ye separate." But with each friend he removed, he brought somebody better into my life.

Read on and find out how God took hold of my life and turned it upside down.

Again I ask, please take my advice. If God has called you, answer him. He will get your attention no matter how much you have to suffer. Just let go, and let him have his way. I can promise you that you will never regret it.

The book of Ecclesiastes says: "To every thing there is a season, and a time to every purpose under heaven: A time to weep, and a time to laugh; a time to mourn, and a time to dance. — *Ecclesiastes 3:1, 4 (KJV)*

I had laughed, and I had danced, when suddenly the seasons began to change. It was now my time to weep.

Somebody somewhere was praying for me, and yes, God was listening.

- . . . The effectual fervent prayer of a righteous man availeth much. — *James 5:16 (KJV)*

I loved God, and I still do. I know that if I had died during my sinful days, it would have been a very sad thing because I believe I was headed straight to hell.

- Therefore to him that knoweth to do good, and doeth it not, to him it is sin. — *James 4:17 (KJV)*

I was going down the wrong road. As I reflect on my past, sometimes I cannot believe how many plans I made. I had plans that were already set in motion. You know the old saying, "You want to make God laugh? Tell him your plans." God must have broken a rib as he listened to me talk about my plans, because in *one* day my whole life changed. If I had any idea what was in store for me on that dreadful day, God knows I would have never gotten out of bed.

Letter Eight
Ready for the Maker's Hands

I had gotten up early on that particular morning. I went through my daily routine of making sure I looked just right before I left for work. I was still very arrogant during that time in my life. Appearances were everything to me. As I dressed for work, the thought that I would not return home the same way never entered my mind.

Later that same day, I was involved in a terrible accident during a training exercise. This accident would leave me permanently disabled for the rest of my life. Accepting the fact that my hand would never be restored was a reality I thought about almost every day.

During the training exercise, my hand got lodged in between a seven-inch metal door. The impact cracked my wrist, and broke my finger in half. After the accident happened, I was devastated to say the least. On a day I never saw coming, I had lost the use of my (dominant) right hand. I was in bad shape. My wrist was crushed in three places. A seven-inch rod was placed inside my wrist, which was held together by six long screws.

This accident was the most painful experience I had ever undergone. The doctor sat me down one day and gave it to me straight. He said I would never again regain the full use of my right hand. I cannot find the words to express the pain that filled my heart after hearing his report.

My life took an immediate turn for the worst. The very things I enjoyed the most, like drawing, playing the keyboard, and fishing were all gone, not to mention my deepest passion, writing. I could no longer write because I could no longer think. Each night I lived in constant pain. The pain was so severe that there were times when I would lose consciousness. As life moved forward, I was at a halt emotionally. Nothing mattered to me anymore, and where in the world were all my friends? It was during that time that God showed me who my true friends were. I had friends who came to see me on a regular basis. Some of my friends cooked for me, while others helped me to stand to my feet when I fell. Each friend gave me the one thing I needed more than anything else, and that was love.

Month after month, I lived in constant pain. Regardless of what medication the doctor gave me, the pain only subsided for a while, and then the throbbing would start all over again. Every night I cried myself to sleep, and every morning the pain woke me up. Anyone that touched me had to be very gentle; the slightest movement brought on even more pain.

Because I am right handed, I had to learn how to train my left hand to do everything. There were days when I was very frustrated. I threw boxes of pens against the wall as I tried to write my own name all over again.

During that time, fear had also taken root in me. My biggest fear was falling, especially in the bathtub. I have always chose bathing over taking a shower. I battled in my mind as to which would be the safest. The one thing I did not want was my cast to become soaked with water, so I decided to bathe.

Life is funny. We fail to realize how many little things we take for granted. Something as simple as getting in and out of the tub alone without any assistance is a blessing. At that time in my life, I had to accept that my life had changed. Getting in and out of the bathtub was a huge task for me. I was still afraid of falling, but God was merciful. He kept reminding me that he was there and would not let go of my hand.

My niece, bless her heart, was very patient with me. She kept reminding me that she would catch me if I fell. I put my trust in her, and eventually I got in and out of the tub without fear.

There were also three women in my life who helped me through the pain. To this day, I consider them the best friends I could have ever hoped to have. In my eyes, it was as if God had sent me some angels. They never forgot me, and they never complained. All they ever did was assist me until I grew strong enough to help myself.

One night I chose to stay at one of my friend's house. Her home was beautiful. She took great pride in keeping things in order. I admired the way she decorated her home. In her master bathroom she had a clam shaped bathtub that I simply adored. The tub looked like it belonged somewhere in a house in Beverly Hills. Her tub was simply awesome. I looked at the beige giant bowl and could not wait to get inside.

Later that night, I asked my friend if I could take a bath. Without hesitation, she ran me a nice warm bath and gave me everything I needed. It never occurred to me that because the inside of the tub was shaped like a bowl, it would be difficult to get out. After my bath, I sat in that tub struggling to get out, but I was too proud to call for help. I opened the drain and allowed all the water to run out, yet I still could not get out. I believe the Lord told my friend that I was in need of help, but did not know how to ask. I sat naked and ashamed because I could not get out of the tub.

After sitting in that empty tub for nearly thirty minutes not knowing what to do, or how to get out, my friend stood on the other side knocking, waiting for me to answer. I could hear the compassion in her voice as she asked if I was okay. I hesitated and turned away. Without saying another word, she walked into the bathroom, reached for a towel, and pulled me out. Not once did she ever make me feel ashamed because I could not help myself. She saw beyond my fault and saw my need.

I needed somebody to help me and God gave me all the help that I needed. He also blessed me with friends who lived in other states. I had two friends who could not be with me because they lived in other states, but they never forgot me. They continued to call and check on me, letting me know that they were there for me. God had surrounded me with loving people who were willing to show me unconditional love, people that knew how to love somebody from the inside out.

As time passed, my pride began to die. I finally admitted to myself that I did not know everything. Each time I looked at my injury, I began to realize that I would never be the same. Some days I cried because I knew my life would also never be the same. It was a very emotional time for me. My life altering completely was the hardest thing to accept. I think that hurt more than my wounds. *Why did this happen to me?* I questioned God every day, but he did not answer me. My eyes were beginning to open in other ways. I finally realized that all the money in the world and all the fame I once cherished meant nothing to me without my health. I learned through my tragedy that health has no price tag on it.

Sometimes late at night when the pain was unbearable, I would remove the bandages and look at the mess that had become of my perfect hand. The bones in my wrist were crushed so bad that the hardware stayed in for months. The pain I felt was real—as real as reality itself. I had to learn to accept something that I had no power to change.

Then the blame came. I needed someone to blame. The one person I blamed for my tragedy was God. He was responsible for my pain. I became angry with him because of what I was going through. I believed he was punishing me for all the sinful things I had done while in New York. It was weird; although I was angry with God, I could not forget God. My mind could not comprehend how God had allowed this to happen to me. There was this voice in my head telling me that God was punishing me.

My niece was so worried about me, she moved in to help take care of me around the clock. Between my niece, my sister and my friends, they were all I had; there was no one else. I needed help preparing my food, cleaning my place, tying my shoes, cutting up my food and the list goes on. It was a scary experience. I was even more afraid of falling and breaking my other hand.

My mental state was slowly declining. I could no longer take my own meds. I had to have my medication administered to me, because I could not remember when I had taken my last pill. In time, my anger with God began to lessen. After months of suffering, I finally repented and asked for his forgiveness. I pleaded with him to take away the pain. I wept before God like a frightened child. No matter how much I cried, God did not remove the pain, but he gave me strength to endure it. Although at the time I was not aware of it, God was purging me.

Each night I cried myself to sleep; I just wanted to die. One particular night I had a dream. In the dream I saw myself walking along a dirt road. As I walked, I saw two puddles of water. One was muddy and the other was clear. As I looked at the muddy water, it reminded me of my life, and what a mess I had made of it. Looking into the muddy water made me more afraid.

All at once, I saw myself crying in my dream. I cried as I looked down at the muddy water pleading with God to forgive me. In a matter of seconds, I could feel my body awakening from sleep. My eyelids were so heavy from the medication. I was fighting the sleep as I faded in and out of consciousness. Then something wonderful happened. *God, the creator of mankind actually spoke to me!* I could hear the sound of his voice as I fought to pull myself from sleep. Although, I could not fully comprehend what was happening, I fought to remain awake. My eyes began slowly opening and closing as I fought to stay awake to hear the audible voice of God.

Although I had never heard his voice, I knew it was God. There is no fear in his presence; there is only peace and joy. He had come to comfort me, and that is exactly what he did. After I was fully awake, I began thinking how merciful God is. I immediately apologized for being angry with him, and begged for his forgiveness.

This is the revelation God gave me during my time of hurt and pain. He allowed me to see the puddles on the side of the road I was traveling. He knew exactly where I was headed, but he also knew how to draw me back into his loving arms. Below are the scriptures God laid on my heart. After reading them, I was at peace just knowing how much he really loved me.

- Before I was afflicted I went astray; but now have I kept thy word.

- It is good for me that I have been afflicted; that I might learn thy statutes.

- They that fear thee will be glad when they see me; because I have hoped in thy word.

- I know, O Lord, that thy judgments are right, and that thou in faithfulness hast afflicted me.

- Let, I pray thee, thy merciful kindness be for my comfort, according to thy word unto thy servant.
  — *Psalm 119:67, 71, 74-76 (KJV)*

The following morning after being in the presence of God, I reached for my Bible, dusted if off, and began to read. Apart from the pain, I read every day and it was not long afterwards that the pain began to decrease. I was reading and praying again. Throughout the day, I began talking to God as I had spoken with him in the past. My hunger for his word was returning and my heart was getting stronger.

One day I read the Bible for nine hours. I started reading around seven in the morning. When I realized the time, it was four in the afternoon. The pain was still present, but with medication, tolerable. As I reflect on my past, I realize that it was through my pain that God had saved me. He was preparing me for my destiny.

Today I am legally disabled. I'll admit I miss having the full use of my hand. My fingers are still locked and will not bend. Why is this infirmity with me? Only God knows. I used to pray day after day that God would release my hand, yet my condition remains unchanged. I believe he left me this way because first of all it keeps me humble, and each time I see the ugly scar that is embedded on the surface of my skin, I remember the past and what could have happened had I not returned to him.

My relationship with the Lord is still growing and I do not have any plans of ever leaving him again. The world has nothing to offer me. Today I see life from a new perspective.

As far as God is concerned, all I can say is: He saved me. He saved me in every way I could possibly be saved. He has kept me safe and continually shows me unconditional love.

After a couple of months passed, the audible voice of the Lord spoke to me again and thanks be to God, I comprehended his every word. Throughout the night, I could feel his omnipotent presence all around me as I drifted off to sleep. But before sleep had completely taken over, I heard the Lord's voice speak words that I will never forget. As I drifted off to sleep, I heard him say, "I love you, my child." Hearing God say that he loved me was worth every moment of agony I had been through. If I never hear his voice again for the rest of my life, I will never forget the hollow sound of his majestic voice, echoing the words "I love you, my child," into my ears.

Letter Nine
Backsliders

Many people look down on backsliders. God says in his word that he is "married to the backslider." You would be surprised how many so-called Christians actually look down on backsliders, but God loves the backslider contrary to what people think.

- Return, ye backsliding children, and I will heal your backsliding. — *Jeremiah 3:22 (KJV)*

- Turn, O backsliding children, saith the Lord; for I am married unto you: and I will take you one of a city, and two of a family, and I will bring you to Zion: — *Jeremiah 3:14 (KJV)*

In order for a person to become a backslider, they had to have gone forward in order to go back. Some people will never become backsliders. They will never take a leap of faith by leaving their comfort zone, and stepping away from the wall they seem to be holding up. They spend their entire life holding up walls with their backs pressed hard against them. These types of people are afraid and unwilling to grow at any cost.

Yes, the backslider fell, but when he fell, he got up again. Some Christians can be so judgmental in terms of the backslider. Yes, he fell, but he got up again! I am not implying that God is pleased if a person lives their entire life as a backslider. That would be agreeing that it is okay to be double-minded. When Christians fall, why not show them love by helping them up? Not beating them down. When I think in terms of a backslider, I think of two types of people; a righteous man and an unrighteous man.

- For though the righteous man falls seven times, they rise again, but the wicked stumble when calamity strikes. — *Proverbs 24:16 (NIV)*

It would seem that an unrighteous man should be falling all the time, but the difference is, when an unrighteous man falls, he shall fall into mischief.

There is a story in the Bible about a man who had two sons in the book of Luke: *A certain man had two sons: And the younger of them said to his father, Father, give me the portion of goods that falleth to me. And he divided unto them his living. And not many days after the younger son gathered all together, and took his journey into a far country, and there wasted his substance with riotous living. And when he had spent all, there arose a mighty famine in that land; and he began to be in want. And he went and joined himself to a citizen of that country; and he sent him into his fields to feed swine. And he would fain (happily) have filled his belly with the husks that the swine did eat; and no man gave unto him. And when he came to himself he said, how many hired servants of my fathers have bread enough and to spare, and I parish with hunger!* — *Luke 15:11-17 (KJV)*

The son thought about all the sin he had committed against his father. He longed to return home to rejoin the father he loved. *He said to himself, I will arise and go to my father, and will say unto him, Father, I have sinned against heaven, and before thee, And am no more worthy to be called thy son: make me as one of thy hired servants. — Luke 15:18-19 (KJV)*

Likewise, when we fall short of the glory of God, our hearts too, long to return to Him. While we wander like lost sheep in an open field, Satan makes us feel condemned by our actions which causes us to believe that God will not accept us back. Now let's see the reaction of the father upon his son's return home: *And he arose, and came to his father. But when he was yet a great way off, his father saw him, and had compassion, and ran and fell on his neck, and kissed him. And the son said unto him, Father, I have sinned against heaven, and in thy sight, and am no more worthy to be called thy son. But the father said to his servants, bring forth the best robe and put it on him; and put a ring on his hand and shoes on his feet; and bring hither the fatted calf, and kill it; and let us eat, and be merry. For this my son was dead, and is alive again; he was lost, and is found. And they began to be merry. — Luke 15:20-24 (KJV)*

The same joy that the father in the story had when he saw his son returning home is the same joy that God has when his children return to him. The father also had an elder son who was not home when his brother returned. Let's see the reaction of the elder brother at hearing the news of his brothers return: *Now his elder son was in the field: and as he came and drew nigh to the house, he heard musick and dancing. And he called one of the servants, and asked what these things meant. And he said unto him, Thy brother is come; and thy father hath killed the fatted calf, because he hath received him safe and sound. And he was angry, and would not go in: therefore came his father out and intreated him. — Luke 15:25-28 (KJV)*

Notice the reaction of the elder son in the story, likewise many Christians respond in this manner. When a Christian who has backslidden returns to God, instead of rejoicing at the return of a brother or sister in Christ, they become jealous of the blessings that God has bestowed upon the backslider. There are many Christians who have been serving the Lord for many years, and have never backslidden once. God can bless who he chooses to bless. We have no control over his decisions. These type of Christians are what I like to refer to as "spiritual giants." They base their belief on the things they do for God. Oftentimes, although not spoken, they secretly hold grudges against their brothers and sisters in Christ, simply because they are being blessed by God. Now, let us look at the father's response to the elder son's reaction, and notice as you read this passage how the eldest son referred to his own brother as not his brother but his father's son: *And he answering said to his father, Lo, these many years do I serve thee, neither transgressed I at any time thy commandment: and yet thou never gavest me a kid, that I might make merry with my friends: But as soon as this thy son was come, which hath devoured thy living with harlots, thou hast killed for him the fatted calf. — Luke 15:29-30 (KJV)*

Could you denote the jealousy of the eldest son and did you also notice how he even refused to call his own flesh and blood his brother, simply because his brother had been forgiven, then blessed by his father? In this same manner, even today, we as Christians carry on in such a way that is simply shameful! Why can't we be happy for one another? Why do so many so-called Christians keep scorecards, keep points, tell everyone about the good things they do for others? Whatever happened to just being happy for someone? In the closing of the story we will now read the father's reaction to his eldest son's behavior: *And he said unto him, Son, thou art ever with me, and all that I have is thine. It was meet that we should make merry, and be glad: for this thy brother was dead, and is alive again; and was lost and is found. — Luke 15:31-32 (KJV)*

That is how God reacts when one of his children returns from the world. He is overjoyed that his child has returned home. Like the father in the story, I am sure our heavenly Father overflows with joy when any of his children return. We should treat the backslider as the father did in the story. After all, sometimes backsliders do come back. And when they do, we should welcome them warmly with open arms.

- Likewise, I say unto you, there is joy in the presence of the angels of God over one sinner that repenteth. — *Luke 15:10 (KJV)*

As Christians, so many of us are so busy trying to convince people how spiritual we are. Whatever happened to sensitivity? When we minister to a brother or a sister in a backslidden condition, we need to remember how to be more sensitive.

I pray and ask God to teach me to practice what I preach. Who am I to look at people who are living in sin? As a Christian I am not supposed to judge that person, but I can judge the sin, but not the person. When I watch the news or read a newspaper I am not someone who believes everything I see or read. The public can be very judgmental, especially with people who have been given a life sentence in prison. As much as you might disagree with me, I strongly believe that not everybody in prison is guilty. It is not my place to judge anyone, that's God's job. My job as a Christian is to see people as God sees them, and learn to love them in spite of what they have done in their life. I do not look at people who have received life sentences and say, "They got just what they deserved." The one thought I always keep in my mind: *Had it not been for the grace of God that could have been me doing time.*

Letter Ten
Love

Loving some people can be difficult at times. I know this statement does not sound very **spiritual**, and I am sorry if I have offended any of the **spiritual giants** who do not battle with anything. But the truth of the matter is, some people are not easy to love. We need God's help to love some people. Jesus demonstrated his love at Calvary. Now he asks that we do our part by loving one another. The majority of the time we will not do something as simple as love one another. Love is an action word, and the Bible clearly states it:

- My little children, let us not love in word, neither in tongue; but in deed and in truth. — *1 John 3:18 (KJV)*

- There is no fear in love; but perfect love casteth out fear: because fear hath torment. He that feareth is not made perfect in love. — *1 John 4:18 (KJV)*

- Greater love hath no man than this, that a man lay down his life for his friends. — *John 15:13 (KJV)*

- Hatred stirreth up strifes: but love covereth all sins. — *Proverbs 10:12 (KJV)*

When Jesus died on the cross, he demonstrated the greatest love by dying for the whole world. He had been beaten by man, and died a brutal death, all for the sake of love. As he hung on the cross and died, his love never failed. With his last few breaths, he prayed:

- Father, forgive them; for they know not what they do. — *Luke 23:34 (KJV)*

Jesus's death was an act of love. His death gave us the opportunity to come boldly to God's throne and find help in our time of need.

- And I say unto you, Ask, and it shall be given you; seek, and ye shall find; knock, and it shall be opened unto you. — *Luke 11:9*

If we would only ask, God would give us new eyes that would allow us to see one another as he sees us, ears to hear the cry of the poor, and a willing heart to answer those cries.

Unfortunately, many people have no idea what love is. The Bible says:

- If I speak in the tongues of men and of angels, but have not love, I am only a resounding gong or a clinging cymbal.

- If I have the gift of prophecy and can fathom all mysteries and all knowledge; and if I have a faith that can move mountains, but have not love, I am nothing.

- If I give all I possess to the poor and surrender my body to the flames, but have not love I gain nothing.

- Love is patient, love is kind, it does not envy, it does not boast, it is not proud.

- It is not rude, it is not self-seeking, it is not easily angered, it keeps no record of wrongs.

- Love does not delight in evil but rejoices with the truth.

- It always protects, always trust, always hopes, always perseveres.

- Now these three remain: faith, hope, and love. But the greatest of these is love. — *1 Corinthians 13:1-7, 13 (NIV)*

- Love worketh no ill to his neighbour: therefore love is the fulfilling of the law. — *Romans 13:10*

Take heed when someone says "I love you," but there is no action behind it. Many people think love is just a feeling. Think again, love requires work. It will take some effort on your part to love somebody.

Lionel Richie wrote a song called "Jesus is Love." Each time I hear that song it makes me realize how blessed I am to have a savior like Jesus. Although all the stories in the Bible are different, the basis of all the stories lead to the same thing, love.

The Bible says love covers a multitude of sins. When you are around sinners, the one thing they are continuingly doing is checking your love meter. I can recall a song that was popular when I was growing up; it was sung by Rockwell. The message in the song was "I always feel like, somebody's watching me." The song was good because it had strong lyrics. Rockwell was speaking the truth, sinners are watching you twenty-four-seven, waiting for that crucial moment when they can say, "Ah ha! Our eyes have seen it! You are no

different than the rest of the hypocrites in the church."
The next phrase that comes pouring out of their mouth is
the famous excuse, "See, that's why I don't go to
church. You're all hypocrites!"

If you walk in love and treat people with kindness
regardless of how evil they may be, they will see the
love of Christ in you. I know this statement to be true
because it was love that saved me.

There are gifted people of God who can talk to
anybody on any level. These people are so in tune with
the spirit of God they know how to talk to others, and
how to listen. Learning to be led by the spirit is
important when ministering to people. A sinner can spot
a fake Christian a mile away. We as Christians have a
great opportunity to affect the lives of many, but not
everyone knows how to handle positions or promotions.

During my military career, I marveled at the
techniques used to hurt soldiers. Cold-hearted sergeants
were given authority over many soldiers. With the
power they possessed, they could have affected
numerous lives in a positive way. Instead, many used
their power for their own self-gratification. The man or
woman who thought they could not accomplish
anything, could have been inspired by the guidance of a
good leader. Instead, they were humiliated, and
disrespected by leaders who simply did not like the way
they looked, or hated the color of their skin. These so-
called *leaders* pollute the souls and minds of decent
people who are simply trying to live the life they have
been given. When people are in positions of power and
have no love or compassion, it is a sad thing. There is no
rest unto the wicked unless they are doing something to

negatively *infect* the life of good, decent people. The Bible says when the righteous are in charge the people rejoice.

Attitude reflects leadership. When a person is placed in a high position, they have an opportunity to make a positive impact on human lives, and that position in itself is a great honor.

I have seen the misuse of power against the feeble from different sides. Many of the sergeants I knew while serving my country, made the life of many soldiers pure hell.

Satan, who is also referred to as the accuser of the brethren, petitions God daily for permission to attack the Christian soldier. Likewise, the sergeants in the military had a similar goal. Their goal was to bring evidence against soldiers whom they wanted gone. Like the snake in the Garden of Eden, these types of sergeants would always start out by befriending the soldiers. While dressed in military fatigues with sergeant stripes or captain bars on their shoulders, they gathered what they called "paper trails" on these unsuspecting soldiers. These leaders would watch soldiers like hawks. Instead of correcting the soldiers, and teaching them the proper way, they would instead keep records of all their wrongs, and stash them away in a file. Again, the soldier would fail. With no clue of what was going on behind closed doors, these same leaders bought beers and told dirty jokes to their prey as they secretly kept notes of all the wrongs of the unsuspecting soldier. After the leaders had gathered enough evidence (paper trails) on the soldier, they would then present the (failures) papers to those in command, who would later impose punishment on the soldier.

What if God treated us that way? Some people really believe that God operates in such a manner. They see him as watching us and waiting for us to make mistakes, so he can send down a bolt of lightning and destroy us. Please remember that God judges the heart. By the heart actions are committed.

Living the life of a Christian is not going to always be easy. The Lord never said it would be easy, but he did say it could be done. God is not the enemy; he is here to love and forgive and save us. Although Satan is keeping paper trails on Christians, and sinners are keeping paper trails on Christians, we must go on. But keep in mind the sinner is watching you from a different perspective. They are watching to see if you really are what you claim to be. Sinners listen to you talk about love and then watch how cruel and hateful you react towards one another. Believe me, somebody is always taking notes on a Christian's behavior, and they have plenty of mental paper.

As Christians we must accept the fact that our lifestyles and our actions will affect how people view God. We must conduct ourselves as children of God by showing love to a world that hates us. It creates an ugly picture when Christians carry on in such ways that are an embarrassment to the Church. How soon we forget that we too were once sinners, saved by grace. We are human just like the rest of the world. God never said we had to pretend that we were incapable of feeling human. I strongly believe that sinners appreciate it when they can see that Christians are human, too, and subject to error. But when we walk around as if we have wings and can fly, they have a hard time relating to us, because in their eyes we have forgotten how hard life can really be without God.

The apostle Paul inspired me a great deal. Paul (from his letters) appeared to be the kind of person who could talk to anybody. He was ready to become anything to gain a soul for Christ. Read what he said:

- For though I be free from all men, yet have I made myself servant unto all, that I might gain the more.

- And unto the Jews I became as a Jew, that I might gain the Jews; to them that are under the law, as under the law, that I might gain them that are under the law;

- To them that are without law, as without law, (being not without law to God, but under the law to Christ,) that I might gain them that are without law.

- To the weak became I as weak, that I might gain the weak: I am made all things to all men, that I might by all means save some.
  — *1 Corinthians 9:19-22*

I believe the whole point of Paul's message is as Christians we need to learn how to minister to unbelievers. Sinners are only doing what they know how to do. First, although you may feel like you are perfect as you stand before a mirror, keep in mind there is no one perfect but a man who died on a cross almost two-thousand years ago. Secondly, stop acting like you were not yourselves once a sinner. Allow people to see that you are a real person with real problems. Here is an example: A sinner comes along and tells you he has a headache. The first thing you do is start preaching as you stand trying to convince him of how the Lord can cure his headache. Most Christians do not know how to communicate with sinners because they are so busy trying to show off their spirituality.

When I was a sinner, I was drawn to Christians who knew how to talk to me, not *at* me. These types of Christians are real people with real problems. They can be bold when they need to be bold, and they can be sensitive when the situation calls for it. They have mastered the wisdom of knowing how to reach out and touch somebody's life. If the truth were to be exposed, in my experience, many Christians who are supposedly giving a testimony about their life are simply bragging. If you really want to help somebody, try loving them first, that is a start.

Letter Eleven
Faith

- Now faith is the substance of things hoped for, the evidence of things not seen. — *Hebrews 11:1 (KJV)*

The key word in this scripture is the word **now**. You need **now** faith to make it today. You cannot live off yesterday's faith and expect to survive in this world. Every morning we need a fresh dose of faith. Everything a Christian believes in centers around faith.

- But without faith it is impossible to please him: for he that cometh to God must believe that is he is, and that he is a rewarder of them that *diligently* seek him. — *Hebrews 11:6 (KJV)*

- Faith comes by hearing and hearing by the word of God. — *Romans 10:17 (KJV)*

You cannot please God without faith. I heard a preacher once (lie) say that a person does not need to go to church. He stood and explained how unimportant going to church was. I knew his words were straight from the pit of hell. It is imperative that you are in a place where you can **hear** the Word of God so your faith can grow. Don't get **now faith** confused with **yesterday's** faith.

No one needs faith for things that have already happened. You need faith for things that have not yet happened. I like to think of faith as fuel in an automobile. Imagine yourself as a car and the fuel is like

78

faith. How long will you be able to run on one fill up? You may be able to travel farther than most cars depending on your engine size, but eventually you will have to stop and refuel, or you will find yourself stranded on the side of the road.

How much faith do we as Christians need according to the book of Matthew?

- . . . If you have faith as a grain of mustard seed, ye shall say unto this mountain, Remove hence to yonder place; and it shall remove; and nothing shall be impossible unto you. — *Matthew 17:20 (KJV)*

You see, faith moves God and I truly believe that it pleases God to see his children walking in faith. No matter what circumstances or situations occur in your life, have faith in God. He will not fail you. Be patient and wait on God. Our time is not his time.

- But, beloved be not ignorant of this one thing, that one day is with the Lord as a thousand years, and a thousand years as one day. — *2 Peter 3:8 (KJV)*

Perhaps you are in a season in your life when you feel as though you have been going through a storm. Have faith in God, trust in him and he will bring it to pass.

The apostles and prophets believed in God's word. Their belief was so strong they were willing to die for it. In fact, many did. Over 50 million Christians were killed because of their faith during the reign of The Roman Empire.

People need ***now faith*** today. The world mocks the Christians—scoffing and laughing at us claiming that God's word is all we have. Well, that type of thinking is okay, because God's word is all we need.

- Knowing this first, that there shall come in the last days scoffers, walking after their own lust.

- And saying, Where is the promise of his coming? for since the fathers fell asleep, all things continue as they were from the beginning of creation. — *2 Peter 3:4 (KJV)*

I challenge you to walk in faith, no matter what the circumstances might be. Make a conscious decision that no matter what you see, you will not be moved. We have God's promise that he will show up, and yes the mountains will move!

In the beginning when the Lord told Noah to build an ark, did you know the river was miles away, and nobody had ever seen rain before? As Noah followed God's instructions by walking in faith, people stood by and laughed at him, and called him mad. But within Noah's heart he chose to trust in God rather than man, therefore he and his entire family were spared.

Like Noah, Abraham also had remarkable faith in God. When asked to offer his beloved son, Isaac to God as a sacrifice, Abraham was obedient to God and did as he was commanded. Abraham was willing to kill his own son because God had asked him to. Because of Abraham's faithfulness, he became the father of many nations. Abraham's faith in God never failed, even unto his dying day.

In my own previous experiences, I had been faced with situations where I saw no way out. I am now convinced that no matter what happens, I will not doubt God's ability to bring me through. As I reflect back on my life long before I was seeking God, he reached his hand out and helped me. It was the summer of 1995, a summer I will never forget. During that summer, I was living on the streets. There was a local shelter that would take me in if the beds were not all filled, but there were nights when I did not make it in time. Like the other homeless people who blow in the wind, I too looked for a cardboard box to lay on and rest. It was a very tough time in my life. Everything around me seemed to be falling apart, but I was determined to keep the faith. In the past it seemed every time my faith was tested, I gave up hope. I could see the tip of my toes touching the Red Sea waiting for God to open it, but like so many times before, fear stepped in. I glanced back at the enemies that were fast approaching and became alarmed by the multitude.

However, a day came in my life when things changed. I looked from all sides and was surrounded by enemies. The only escape for me was the Red Sea. I was determined not to run again. I stood on the brink of the shoreline and began to praise God no matter how close the enemy approached. Suddenly, like a bolt of lightning in the sky, God's word came through, commanding the sea to open and let me pass. God cannot fail! If God is for you, who can be against you?

Letter Twelve
Temptation

- There hath no temptation taken you but such as is common to man: but God is faithful, who will not suffer you to be tempted above that ye are able; but will with the temptation also make a way to escape, that ye may be able to bear it.
  — *1 Corinthians 10:13 (KJV)*

If you are honest with yourself, each time you are faced with temptation, there is always a way out. But because temptation is forever present, waiting for the right moment to entice us, it is beneficial for us to stay in God's presence. Remember, with God all things are possible.

Jesus knew temptation would try to deceive us. Even he was tempted of the devil for forty days and forty nights. He showed us by his refusal to give in to Satan that we too could become conquerors.

The devil never takes a day off, and neither should we. He is always lurking around waiting for the right moment when we are most vulnerable. Jesus knew the devil's plan and left us warnings about temptation because he knew what damage temptation could do if we yield to it.

- Watch therefore that ye enter not into temptation: the spirit indeed is willing, but the flesh is weak.
  — *Matthew 26:41 (KJV)*

There is a struggle going on inside of us. The spirit and the physical man are in constant war with one another. We need spiritual food and prayer to keep our flesh under subjection.

The first temptation began in the Garden of Eden. In the beginning, after God created all things, he created man.

- And the Lord God formed man of the dust of the ground, and breathed into his nostrils the breath of life; and man (Adam) became a living soul. — *Genesis 2:7 (KJV)*

- And the Lord God said, It is not good that the man should be alone; I will make him an help meet for him.

- And the Lord God caused a deep sleep to fall upon Adam, and he slept: and he took one of his ribs, and closed up the flesh instead thereof;

- And the rib, which the Lord God had taken from man, made he a woman, and brought her unto the man.

- And Adam said, This is now bone of my bones, and flesh of my flesh: she shall be called Woman, because she was taken out of Man. — *Genesis 2:18, 21-23 (KJV)*

God created a beautiful garden for the man and his wife, called the Garden of Eden. The garden was a place where both the man and his wife lived. It was their home. God gave both the man and the woman specific instruction:

- And the Lord God commanded the man, saying, Of every tree of the garden thou mayest freely eat:

- But of the tree of the knowledge of good and evil, thou shalt not eat of it: for in the day that you eatest thereof thou shalt surely die. — *Genesis 2:16-17 (KJV)*

One day while in the garden, Eve was tempted by that old serpent the devil. The devil stood beside a tree and whispered lies into her ear. The more she listened, the stronger Satan's words took root in her heart. In the end, temptation was aroused and she took of the fruit and ate.

Adam came along and saw what his wife had done. The right thing for him to do was not to partake of his wife's doings, but instead he too was tempted and ate as well. Although both the man and his wife were commanded not to eat of the tree of the knowledge of good and evil, they willingly disobeyed God and yielded to temptation.

- Therefore the Lord God sent him forth from the Garden of Eden, to till the ground from whence he was taken. — *Genesis 3:23 (KJV)*

Temptation is always present, always waiting for a moment when we are most vulnerable. In spite of what the world says, temptation does not come from God, it comes from man's own lust, giving way for the devil to come in and persuade man to sin.

- Let no man say when he is tempted, I am tempted of God: for God cannot be tempted with evil, neither tempteth he any man:

- But ***every man is tempted***, when he is ***drawn away of his own lust, and enticed.***

- Then when lust hath conceived, it bringeth forth sin; and sin, when it is finished, bringeth forth death. — *James 1:13-15 (KJV)*

Have you ever been faced with a situation where you felt tempted? Perhaps there is a supervisor at work who rides your back at every opportunity. Your heart races inside your chest as he harshly speaks to you, your pulse increases, and the one thing you wish you could do is bring him bodily harm, or at least tell him exactly what you think of him. You stand wishing you could do something, but something triggers in your brain *repercussions*. What about the repercussions?

I am sure Judas, after receiving those thirty pieces of silver thought about the repercussions, but it was too late for him. Temptation had already taken root in his heart, and in the end, he was not able to live with the guilt, and ended up taking his own life. It was all a set up, but because Judas was blinded by his own greed he could not see past his own selfish desire.

We look at temptation and the first thought that crosses our mind is sexual sin. Temptation comes in all shapes and forms. It covers a vast area of transgressions, from murder, stealing, lying, adultery, disobedience, lustful eyes, greed, and betrayal just to a name a few. Two of the easiest ways for temptation to get in is through our thoughts.

When I was in my teens, like most teenagers, temptation was all around me. I had a so-called boyfriend at the time. He did everything to try to convince me that sex before marriage was okay.

Finally, after months of his constant begging, I gave in to him, but in the midst of the heated moment I told him to stop. As his hands roamed over me, I began to think about all my friends who were teen mothers, and to be honest, he just was not worth it. Of course he was upset, and would not speak to me for weeks, but that was okay with me. I still had my self-respect, and my virginity. On the day I was finally married, (to a different man of course) I wore a white wedding gown representing every woman who had kept her virginity until her wedding day and it felt so good as I wore it.

Temptation *always* begins with a thought. In my lifetime, I have known people personally who have sworn they would never commit adultery, but that was before temptation showed up. I must stress this again; ***temptation always begins with a thought***. Thoughts lead to fantasizing. Before you realize it, your body begins to yearn for just a simple touch of a hand. Your emotions feel like someone has just turned up the eye on the stove. Oh, if I could just have one kiss, not realizing that one kiss can lead to something else. I am sure during those times, a moment of escape was there showing you a way out, but your mind was already made up. The temptation was strong and your body was ready for something to happen. The book of Proverbs says:

- Let thy fountain be blessed: and rejoice with the wife of your youth. — *Proverbs 5:18 (NIV)*

- Lust not after her beauty in thine heart; neither let her take thee with her eyelids.

- For by means of a whorish woman a man is brought to a piece of bread: and the adulteress will hunt for the precious life.

- Can a man take fire in his bosom, and his clothes not be burned?

- Can one go upon hot coals, and his feet not be burned?

- So he that goeth in to his neighbor's wife; whosoever toucheth her shall not be innocent.
— *Proverbs 6:25-29 (KJV)*

- Flee fornication. Every sin that a man doeth is without the body; but he that committeth fornication sinneth against his own body.

- What? know ye not that your body is the temple of the Holy Ghost which is in you, which ye have of God, and ye are not your own?
— *1 Corinthians 6:18-19 (KJV)*

Letter Thirteen
Can You Hear Me?

For centuries man has desired to hear the audible voice of God. Some people have heard his voice audibly, including me, while others have not. If you will only listen, you will hear him speaking, but you say, "I cannot hear him."

Imagine you are on a crowded street, the sound of loud automobiles race past your ears intermixed with the chatter of many other voices. There in the midst of the crowd Jesus stands calling out to you, but because of the cares of this world your mind remains fixed on all that surrounds you, and you cannot hear him. Again, he calls out to you, yet you still cannot hear his voice.

Although God created us for his glory, most people have no knowledge of him, neither can they recognize the sound of his voice, and therefore continually walk in darkness and say: "I cannot hear God's voice."

- And when he putteth forth his own sheep, he goeth before them, and the sheep follow him; for they know his voice.

- And a stranger will they not follow, but will flee from him: for they know not the voice of strangers. — *John 10:4-5 (KJV)*

Do you think God is not speaking? He is speaking to the world every day, yet the world cannot hear him, nor can they recognize his voice. Even in the womb, God knows all about you, He formed man and created him in his own image, yet man cannot hear God when he calls him by name.

God's voice speaks even from creation, so man is without excuse. The great mountains and deep oceans declare his presence. Like roaring thunder that fills the sky before a storm, God's voice echoes into the heart of every man, yet many cannot hear him.

- Behold, I stand at the door, and knock: if any man hear my voice, and open the door, I will come in to him, and will sup with him, and he with me. — *Revelation 3:20 (KJV)*

The Lord desires to know us, and instructs us to keep his commandments. But how can you know him when you will not seek him? God will draw closer to you as you draw closer to him. God is not a man that he can lie. He is a spirit, a spirit of never ending truth. But the world has complicated God's love.

Men with worldly knowledge have sought to find the meaning of God. They want to know who he is, and where he comes from. Scientists have tried to explain God's existence; they have tried to imitate the sound of his voice in movies, imitate his power by wolves in sheep's clothing. Yet they cannot hear him, nor can they understand his ways because they are of this world.

Do you know the power of words? With *words* God created the world. He spoke everything into existence. As you listen to the multitude of voices in the world, it is very important that above all things you guard your heart. It is with the heart you will believe.

- Call unto me, and I will answer thee, and shew thee great and mighty things, which thou knowest not. — *Jeremiah 33:3 (KJV)*

Can you hear God's voice? Even now he is speaking, yet you say you cannot hear him.

Letter Fourteen
Unforgiveness

No matter how difficult it may be, you must forgive one another. When we refuse to forgive, we tie God's hands so he cannot help us. In the book of Matthew Jesus prayed:

- For if you forgive men their trespasses, your heavenly Father will also forgive you:

- But if ye forgive not men their trespasses, neither will your Father forgive your trespasses.
  — *Matthew 6:14-15 (KJV)*

- Then came Peter to him, and said, Lord, how oft shall my brother sin against me, and I forgive him? till seven times?

- Jesus saith unto him, I say not unto thee, Until seven times: but, Until seventy times seven.
  — *Matthew 18:21-22 (KJV)*

Forgiveness is essential when walking with God. We give life to sin by harboring feelings of hate and unforgiveness. Unforgiveness is like an invisible root growing inside the heart. Everything that has life in it has roots, and roots can grow very deep. When you choose not to forgive others, you leave your heart open to grow bad roots. Bad roots attach themselves throughout your body causing sickness, and sometimes death. When you refuse to forgive others you are not imprisoning them, it is you who will serve the sentence. You become the prisoner because you carry the chains of bondage. Your hands and feet become bound; blessings from heaven are withheld, and your prayers go unanswered, because you refuse to forgive.

- Moreover if thy brother shall trespass against thee, go and tell him his fault between thee and him alone: if he shall hear thee, thou hast gained thy brother.

- But if he will not hear thee, then take with thee one or two more, that in the mouth of two or three witnesses every word may be established.

- And if he shall neglect to hear them, tell it unto the church: but if he neglect to hear the church, let him be unto thee as an heathen man and a publican. — *Matthew 18:15-17 (KJV)*

When you forgive someone you are setting your own heart free. You will be free to love, free to forgive, and free to receive. A tightly closed fist will hold anything securely, but be wise and know that as surely as nothing gets out, nothing gets in. When we refuse to forgive, we are holding back the love. Open your heart to someone who has hurt you and learn to forgive.

"To error is human, but to forgive is divine."

Make a promise to yourself that no matter what people do or say, refuse to become a prisoner and allow them forgiveness. God has already made it clear, if you do not forgive others, he will not forgive you. I know it is hard to forgive someone who has hurt you, but the best advice I can give anyone during those times is to remember the cross. Remember Calvary and all that Jesus did when he died for you and me.

Unforgiveness is like a disease. It eats away at you until all your compassion is gone, leaving you with nothing but bitterness inside. It will rob you like a thief in the night, keep you sick, and fill your heart with calluses. If your heart remains in a state of unforgiveness too long, you will find it almost impossible to love.

I am aware that most people view Christians as people who do not struggle with much of anything. I beg to differ. Christians struggle with sin and unforgiveness like everybody else. You may not be aware of it, but they do. According to God's word in John 8:32, the truth will not *set* you free, but *make* you free. Today I will reveal yet another truth.

There was a time when I struggled with unforgiveness. A wise man gave me a suggestion to my problem, which eventually helped me overcome. He said, "If you truly want to be able to forgive someone, humble yourself before God, and pray each day that God will bless that person. Thereby your love will prevail, and the root of unforgiveness will be destroyed!"

I am not going to lie and tell you that what this man was asking of me was easy. Praying for God to bless someone who had practically torn my heart out was not easy the first time around. It took quite a few tries before I could even utter the words "bless them Father." My flesh wanted God to send a tornado against their home, or break a bone or two. After I found the strength to pray for my enemies, in time God released me from the feelings of resentment. I was then free to love my enemies in spite of their transgressions. If we love Jesus, we will keep his commandments. One of his greatest commandments is that we love one another, even as he loved us.

As faith without works is dead, in my opinion love without action is also dead. I believe Jesus knew that we would need help in the area of forgiveness, that is why he prayed this prayer to the Father: "And forgive us our sins; for we also forgive every one that is indebted to us . . ." — *Luke 11:4 (KJV)*

No matter what you do in your life, you must learn to forgive. Tomorrow is not promised. What will you gain after discovering someone you loved has passed away, and you did not get the chance to say, "I forgive you" or "Forgive me."

Letter Fifteen
Battles of the Mind

The mind is a powerful weapon. We must be cognitive of everything we allow to enter into it. Think of the mind in terms of a bank. As we watch television, read a newspaper, or do something as simple as ponder ideas and/or situations, we are making deposits into our minds.

Thoughts fill our brain every second of the day. The devil uses our mind to control our behavior, and our thoughts. God gives us specific instructions on how to protect our minds. One way of protecting our minds is by putting on the helmet of salvation *(Ephesians 6:14)*. Imagine the devil standing by all day shooting arrows (thoughts) into your mind. Contrary to what you might have been told, you **can** decide on what things to think about. We can train our mind to think of anything we choose. Like a bank, we must be trained to detect counterfeits when we sense them trying to enter into our thoughts.

I can recall a summer spent in New York City. I was in my early teens at the time. Being young and naïve, I made a terrible mistake. I gave a vendor a fifty-dollar bill in exchange for some merchandise he was selling. If my memory served me correctly, the item I purchased was five-dollars to be exact. I told him I did not have anything smaller than a fifty-dollar bill, which I held before him and asked if he could break it. I will never forget how his eyes shimmered as he looked at that crispy bill. A tiny smile appeared at the corner of his mouth as he quickly ran his hand into his pocket and pulled out a seemingly large roll of twenty-dollar bills. I stood waiting for the remaining five-dollars, which he took from his other pocket and passed it to me. After I received my change, I walked away and intermixed into the crowded street filled with tourists.

Following that encounter, I would say a good twenty minutes had past, when suddenly I spotted an office supply store ahead. I stepped inside and began shopping for a few items. Once I had everything I needed, I headed for the checkout. The cashier rung up my items and told me the total. I quickly reached into my pocket and pulled the remaining money out that I had received from the vendor. Much to my surprise as I pulled a twenty from my pocket, it ripped in half! My first thought was, *I need some tape.* I looked at the cashier in sort of an embarrassing way. I then tried the next twenty, but on my second attempt, she pulled out a money-marking pen, which caused me to think she had smelled something fishy. The cashier had a good eye, it was apparent she knew money, and knew it well. She then stroked the bill with the marker. I had no idea what she was doing until she remarked, "This money is fake!"

"Fake? That's twenty bucks, lady!" I stated.

"Yeah, it's a twenty all right," she added. "But it is not real."

The first face that flashed through my mind was the vendor. I was furious! The man I had given my money to had tricked me by giving me counterfeit money. I ran charging out of the store thinking he would still be on that same corner, but of course, he was long gone.

That vendor got the best of me because I did not have a trained eye to spot a fake bill. The signs were there, but I was not skilled enough about counterfeit money. A stranger had taken advantage of me and taught me a valuable lesson. Unfortunately, it cost me fifty-dollars, but it was a lesson that I will never forget.

Our minds work in a similar way. Satan comes along and puts all kinds of mental pictures in our heads. The majority of the time if we are not trained to see a counterfeit thought, we conceive it as being real.

The Bible speaks about how our thoughts can become our enemies. We must be careful what we choose to think. When I was a kid, my mother used to say: "An idle mind is the devil's workshop." A thought can be just as sinful as the act.

- But I say unto you, That whosoever looketh upon a woman to lust after her hath committed adultery with her already in his heart. — *Matthew 5:28 (KJV)*

Looking can lead to thinking and thinking can lead to doing. We have a right to decide what thoughts we think. Our thoughts are powerful and we must be careful of the ideas we deposit into our minds.

- And you, that were sometime alienated and enemies in your mind by wicked works, yet now hath he reconciled. — *Colossians 1:21 (KJV)*

I realize this may be hard for many of you to digest, but you really can control your thought life. You do not have to sit by and accept every thought that passes through your mind. We can control our thoughts, but the question is how? How can we really control our thought

97

life? Let us see what advice the word of God says concerning our thoughts.

- For though we walk in the flesh, we do not war after the flesh:

- (For the weapons of our warfare are not carnal, but mighty through God to the pulling down of strong holds;)

- Casting down *imaginations*, and every high thing that exalteth itself against the knowledge of God, and bringing into captivity every *thought* to the obedience of Christ:
  — *2 Corinthians 10:3-5 (KJV)*

According to the scripture listed above, we have hope! Not only do we have hope, we have evidence based on God's word that we can control our thought life. You do not have to accept counterfeits any longer. Be cautious of what you allow into your mind.

Thoughts enter through any door they can find. Watching and believing what we see on television is one of the easiest ways of getting inside our mind, but it is not the only way. Having an innocent conversation with someone can provoke certain thoughts. You cannot talk to everybody about everything. As they speak, they are dropping seeds into your mind. If you are not mature enough to distinguish between real or fake thoughts, you may become a victim of someone else's thought life. Movies, television, and media can be very entertaining, just be sure of who is entertaining you as you are watching the world's entertainment.

Letter Sixteen
The Red Sea

- And we know that all things work together for good to them that love God, to them who are the called according to his purpose.
  — *Romans 8:28 (KJV)*

Do you really understand what those words mean? It means that God can take a very bad situation and turn it completely around. When the children of Israel were trapped against the Red Sea their situation seemed hopeless. There was no way of escape, or so it seemed. It may seem strange to you, but their situation was really a good thing. It seemed impossible that anyone could escape, but look what happened: God opened the sea and allowed the children of Israel to walk on dry land! He could not have performed such a miracle if they were not in need of help. God also purposely hardened Pharaoh's heart so he would pursue the Israelites after they left Egypt.

Because I was ignorant of God's word, I thought the act of God doing such a thing was cruel. He sent Moses to Pharaoh with the intention of hardening his heart, so he would not let the Hebrews go. I could not understand why the Lord would put Moses in such a bad position after commanding him to go to Egypt. Suddenly, the answer was revealed to me: God is a strategic God! He actually likes it when things seem impossible. It is when we are at our weakest, that his strength is made perfect. That is how God gets his glory. So if you are in a bad situation begin to praise God. When praises go up, blessings come down. If your situation seems impossible, that is even better. I know it sounds crazy, but that is how God operates. He fixes things we consider impossible. In the eyes of man it may seem impossible, but for God, all things are possible.

Moses trusted God. The Hebrews could not see a way out; they felt trapped. But Moses already knew God's plan. He knew in his heart that there was no way God was going to abandon them and allow them to fall into Pharaoh's hands again.

Right now at this very moment in your life, you may be standing between the Red Sea and some man's army. The situation may seem hopeless. Your Pharaoh might be your landlord or the electric company threatening to turn off your lights. Maybe you have just found out you are being laid off and have mouths to feed. No matter what the situation is, believe God and stand on his word. He will command the sea to open for you and allow you to pass through on dry ground, if you will only stand on his word. Be bold, unmovable, and stubborn each time the devil tells you there is no hope. God is our hope! He is our redeemer, and *his word will never return to him void, but will accomplish that which He pleases, and it shall prosper in the thing where unto it is sent.* — *Isaiah 55:11 (KJV)*

Perhaps you have said I have done all I can do, still nothing has happened. God knew the day would come when you would be faced with situations such as the ones you are going through. That is why it is so important to read about the prophets in the Bible. Their stories of struggle and triumph were written to encourage our faith. Sometimes things may become so unbearable you may need to cry. If you need to cry, go ahead and cry. Afterwards arise to your feet and do what God has commanded. Be obedient to his word and when you have done all to stand, stand therefore!

- Wherefore take unto you the whole armor of God, that ye may be able to withstand in the evil day, and having done all, to stand.

- Stand therefore, having your loins girt about with truth, and having on the breastplate of righteousness; — *Ephesians 6:13-14 (KJV)*

- Be on your guard; stand firm in the faith; be men of courage; be strong. — *1 Corinthians 16:13 (NIV)*

Like you, the Hebrews felt trapped, they could see no way out. But I am here to tell you, God will make a way when there is no way! Stand and watch as God makes a way in the middle of the sea for you so you can walk through in victory! All the glory and all the praise belongs to the Lord. Trust in him with your whole heart.

- . . . for he hath said, I will never leave thee, nor forsake thee.

- So that we may boldly say, The Lord is my helper, and I will not fear what man shall do unto me. — *Hebrews 13:5-6 (KJV)*

- Wait on the Lord: be of good courage, and he shall strengthen thine heart: wait, I say, on the Lord. — *Psalm 27:14 (KJV)*

- But my God shall supply all your need according to his riches in glory by Christ Jesus. — *Philippians 4:19 (KJV)*

Letter Seventeen
I Was Born Like This!

How did this "being gay thing" happen? Can we agree that everything God made is good? Many people take the word "good" and run with it. Immediately they take the word "good" and dissect it. We become confused in attempting to place the word where it really applies. The Bible clearly states that everything God made was good.

God created us in his image. When a child is born, he or she is born into a world of sin and later becomes a sinner. People struggle daily with our emotions because sin is all around us. Paul stated it so beautifully in the book of Romans.

- We know that the law is spiritual; but I am unspiritual, sold as a slave to sin.

- I do not understand what I do. For what I want to do I do not do, but what I hate, I do.

- And if I do what I do not want to do, I agree that the law is good.

- As it is, it is no longer I myself who do it, but it is sin living in me.

- I know that nothing good lives in me, that is, in my sinful nature. — *Romans 7:14-18 (NIV)*

Romans 7:21-25 further states, "So I find this law at work: When I want to do good, evil is right there for me. For in my inner being I delight in God's law; but I see another law at work in the members of my body, waging war against the law of my mind and making me a prisoner of the law of sin at work within my members. What a wretched man I am! Who will rescue me from this body of death? Thanks be to God—through Jesus Christ our Lord!"

Reading this passage helped me understand that Paul also understood how hard it often is to do the right things even when you really want to. My favorite part of this passage is what Paul later stated in Romans 8:1-4 (NIV): "Therefore, there is now no condemnation for those who are in Christ Jesus, because through Christ Jesus the law of the Spirit of life set me free from the law of sin and death. For what the law was powerless to do in that it was weakened by the sinful nature, God did by sending his own Son in the likeness of sinful man to be a sin offering. And so he condemned sin in sinful man, in order that the righteous requirements of the law might be fully met in us, who do not live according to the sinful nature but according to the Spirit."

There is a struggle going on in a lot of us, and that is all the sin that constantly surrounds us. We have hope each time we pray to the Father in the name of Jesus. When God made man he used a special ingredient, an ingredient that separated us from everything else he made. God made man with a soul and a will to choose.

- And if it seem evil unto you to serve the Lord, choose you this day whom ye will serve; whether the gods which your fathers served that were on the other side of the flood, or the gods of the Amorites, in whose land ye dwell: but as for me

and my house we will serve the Lord.
— *Joshua 24:15 (KJV)*

If you choose God, you must be willing to follow his Commandments and become a disciple of Jesus Christ. There is no wonder why so many souls are misled when making a choice between God and Satan. We walk around without a clue of reality.

Man will not live forever in this physical body. In the beginning before Adam and Eve sinned, God had great plans for us, but after their disobedience occurred, sin was born into the world and began to run free into the hearts of men.

- So God created man in his own image, in the image of God created he him; male and female created he them.

- And God blessed them, and God said unto them, Be fruitful and multiply, and replenish the earth and subdue it: . . . — *Genesis 1:27-28 (KJV)*

Every time God creates something beautiful, the devil comes along and tries to pervert its natural use. Most homosexuals are not convicted of their lifestyle, and couldn't care less about going to hell. That is mainly because they have a reprobate mind. Comedians make fun of gay people all the time, especially the gay guy. We know that some comedians will do anything for a laugh at the expense of anyone. People really enjoy laughing at the gay man who seems to amuse many with his feminine mannerisms and girlish ways of expressing himself.

We should start by getting some facts straight in terms of homosexuality. Homosexuality has been around for centuries. It did not just start a decade ago. It has been around a very long time.

The shame of homosexuality has driven many people to suicide, drugs, and living a life of denial. The biggest lie the devil has spread in the world today is, "You were born like that." Tell me. When was the last time you saw a gay baby?

We really do live in two worlds. We are spiritual beings living in a fleshly body. God created the world for man, and hell for the devil and his angels. However, because people have turned their backs on God, refusing to acknowledge him, he has given many over to a reprobate mind.

Now, on the other hand, there are some Christians who play a big part in making homosexuals feel unwanted and unloved. When a homosexual does turn to God, they need the support of the church. Instead of getting support, they are isolated from the masses, and thus they return to the world from where they came.

From the research I have done in searching out the scriptures, I have gained some insight into the gay world. I want to attempt to explain to the best of my knowledge how this perverted spirit operates in the life of man, and how it gets inside of a person. I hope while reading this chapter, you will not assume that I am attempting to challenge your intelligence by my constant clarifying of certain terms. Please keep in mind that some of my readers may not be as educated as you are on this subject, and may need a little more insight. Some of the terminology I use may seem a little confusing to some of you, but try to follow as I attempt to explain homosexuality from a spiritual point of view.

According to the Bible, it is considered perversion when you use something (like sex) for other than what it was created for, such as people having sex with the same gender. People pervert sex and God's word when they commit these acts. Although you may not be aware of it, there are two worlds, one is spirit and one is flesh. Unclean spirits travel throughout the earth in search of a home (body). When this perverted spirit finds a body, it dwells inside of a person for as long as they are welcomed to remain.

This spirit can take residence as early as the age of six or seven years. Take some time and read the story of a child who was possessed with an evil spirit. — *Matthew 17:14-20 (KJV)*

Read the story for yourself so you can see that evil spirits can possess children; they will find a home in anyone they can. As the child grows, this spirit of perversion stays with the child as he matures. Contrary to popular opinion, I believe a parent is always the first to know when their child is displaying homosexual behavior. Most parents are not sure of what to do, so they secretly pray their child will someday grow out of it.

By the time the child is a teenager, he is then convinced that he is gay, but because of the shame he feels, he keeps it to himself, or as the world calls it, "in the closet." As the child grows, the devil shoots perverted thoughts into his mind all day long. These thoughts (arrows) filled with sexual immorality and feelings for the same sex run through his mind uncontrollably.

A little boy discovers he cannot stop thinking about another boy in his class. He cannot understand what is happening to him, but the last thing he wants to be labeled as, is a fag or a homo. The tragedy occurs when a mother finds her child unable to cope with the monster growing inside of him, and he ends up committing suicide. When I hear of a child or an adult who has committed suicide because they hated what they were, it breaks my heart. The person who commits suicide because of their shame, grew to hate themselves and the perverted feelings they could not control. Many Christians do not help by telling them they are going to bust hell wide open.

Allow me to expose some light so we can see the truth. God hates "all" sin. For some reason the world treats homosexuals as if they are the worst people in the world. People, please stop! Homosexuals, transsexuals, and people with gender issues are dying every day because of this lie. God does not hate people; he hates "sin," not people. It saddens me to know that even as I write these words, somewhere in the world somebody is contemplating suicide because some jerk has convinced them they are better off dead.

You do not have to agree with their lifestyle, love them in spite of how they live. Accept a simple fact: You cannot change people. The only thing you are going to do is drive them away and further into the devil's arms. The best thing you can do is pray.

My desire is to see the gay man and the gay woman find God. Somebody needs to tell them that God loves them! He does not love what you are doing, but he loves the soul living inside of you. You might feel like you cannot change what you are. Nevertheless, you are wrong; God can change anybody. Look around you, and begin to focus on people who have changed. The alcoholic has put down the bottle, the drug addict has thrown away the pipe and needle and you too can change if you really want to.

The world is no more than a game of soul winning. In the end, God is going to put an end to all this sinning in the world. Soon Jesus will return to claim all that are his. When he returns, will he find you doing something that will bring you shame?

Somebody is praying for your salvation. Yet no one is going to force you to change your ways. We are all passing through the world; none of us are here to stay. Before the end comes, the devil wants to take as many souls as he can to his final destination, which is, The Lake of Fire!

I know for many of you this is a big pill to swallow, but if I only reach one person by writing these words, my words were not in vain. The world tells you how much of a disgrace you are, but very few tell you how loved you are and how you can be free of this lifestyle.

- Above all things have intense and unfailing love for one another, for love covers a multitude of sins. — *1 Peter 4:8 (AMP)*

The only thing God wants from you is honesty. Tell him the truth. Tell God how much you enjoy your lifestyle. Yes, you read that correct. You see God already knows how much you enjoy what you are doing. Tell him. Go to him and tell him the truth. Ask him to take the perverted spirit that is in control of your body and your life out of you. God has placed ministers, prophets, evangelists, teachers and Christians who have been trained in God's word. They are soldiers in the army of the Lord and God has chosen them to feed his sheep and watch over his lambs. I also want to clarify that God is omnipotent, meaning he is everywhere at all times. He will hear you if you cry out from your bedroom or from a corner on a street. All he wants is to save you.

Hollywood, on the other hand, is doing a great job of convincing the world that being gay is okay. But they do not tell you that once your life on earth has ended, a terrible fate awaits you.

In the past, I attended a funeral of a friend whom I knew was gay. Sadly, he had not accepted Jesus as his Savior. I cannot begin to tell you how brokenhearted I was. I listened as one person after another stood up and said that he was in a better place. The more I listened, the more I wanted to stand up and scream, "Liar! Liar!"

It was too late for my friend, he had made his choice and there was no second chance for him. I promised myself I would try to reach someone who still had life in them and would tell them about Jesus Christ. Please, take heed to God's word and invite Jesus into your life before it is too late. Although I do not know you personally, my heart is with you, and I am praying for you to find the truth.

You may not be aware of the story of the rainbow in connection with the gay world. Did you know that the rainbow is a symbol of a covenant (a promise) made by God? You are not alone if you did not know the real story behind rainbows. I myself did not know the meaning until I read the book of Genesis for myself. Let us see how God feels about rainbows:

- And God spake unto Noah, and to his sons with him, saying,

- And I, behold, I establish my covenant with you, and with your seed after you;

- And with every living creature that is with you, of the fowl, of the cattle, and of every beast of the earth with you; from all that go out of the ark, to every beast of the earth.

- And I will establish my covenant with you, neither shall all flesh be cut off any more by the waters of a flood, neither shall there any more be a flood to destroy the earth.

- And God said, This is the token of the covenant which I make between me and you and every living creature that is with you, for perpetual generations:

- I do set *my bow in the cloud*, and it shall be for a token of a covenant between me and the earth;

- And it shall come to pass, when I bring a cloud over the earth, that the bow shall be seen in the cloud:

- And I will remember my covenant, which is between me and you and every living creature of all flesh; and the waters shall no more become a flood to destroy all flesh.

- And the bow shall be in the cloud; and I will look upon it, that I may remember the ***everlasting covenant*** between God and every living creature of all flesh that is upon the earth. — *Genesis 9:8-16 (KJV)*

Now, if you did not know the story of rainbows, now you know. Rainbows are very holy to God. Have you partaken in using his rainbow to represent your life style? Wake up people! If you are a homosexual, now that you know the truth, how can you use God's beautiful rainbow to signify a lifestyle that he considers an abomination?

I have told you the truth and instructed you where you can read these scriptures for yourself. The choice is up to you. I hope you choose life. These are the words of the Lord concerning homosexuality, not mine.

- Do you not know that the unrighteous and the wrongdoers will not inherit or have any share in the kingdom of God? Do not be deceived (misled): neither the impure and immoral, nor idolaters, nor adulterers, nor those who participate in homosexuality, — *1 Corinthians 6:9 (AMP)*

- You shall not lie with a man as with a woman; it is an abomination. — *Leviticus 18:22 (AMP)*

- For this reason God gave them over and abandoned them to vile affections and degrading passions. For their women exchanged their natural function for an unnatural, and abnormal one,

- And the men also turned from natural relations with women and were set ablaze with lust for one another—men committing shameful acts with men and suffering in their own bodies and personalities the inevitable consequences and penalty of their wrong-doing and going astray. Which was their fitting retribution.

- And so, since they did not see fit to acknowledge God or approve of Him or consider Him worth the knowing, God gave them over to a based and condemned mind, to do things not proper or decent, but loathsome. — *Romans 1:26-28 (AMP)*

Please understand dear one, I am not making this up. These scriptures are from the word of God. You may feel that you have found someone who is worth going to hell for, but perhaps maybe no one has ever told you of the torments that await those in hell. Living a homosexual lifestyle is a temporary fix for happiness. Right now, you may feel like you are in heaven on earth in the arms of your lover. However, the day will come when you will have to give an account for your lifestyle. Take a moment and ask yourself, is a moment of temporary pleasure worth a lifetime in hell?

I have decided to close this chapter with some of the lies the devil uses to deceive those living a homosexual lifestyle. See how many excuses you can recall hearing as you read them. Perhaps even you have a few of these excuses buried in your own heart.

Excuses:

1. I sleep with the same sex sometimes, but that doesn't mean I'm a homo. I'm bi.

2. This is my life and I'm not going to let anybody tell me how to live it.

3. We created our own flag; it reflects people of all colors!

4. I didn't ask to be born. This is who I am. I just wish people would accept it.

5. It doesn't matter if your family hates you; we're your family now, and we love you.

6. I will never come out of the closet. I see how the world treats gays, no thanks.

7. Gays love gays. Be proud of what you are; we have no reason to be ashamed!

8. There is nothing wrong with marriage between two people of the same sex.

9. The only thing that matters is that we love each other, and should be allowed to marry.

10. We want the same rights as everybody else. Why can't we adopt children?

11. In time the world will accept us, because we're not going anywhere, so just accept it.

12. Did I ever try to tell you who to love? So why are you trying to tell me who to love?

13. I'm thinking of having a sex change operation because I feel trapped in this body.

14. My lover and I have been together for 25 years, if that's not love, what is it?

15. God made me, so if I'm not the right sex, it's his fault. He knew I wanted to be a girl.

16. People think being gay is just about sex; it is about being with someone you really love.

17. I was born gay and there's nothing I can do to change that; this is who I am.

18. I know what the Bible says about gays, but don't you know the Bible was written by man?

19. God is not going to send me to hell because of who I choose to love. I'm a good person.

20. I have thought of killing myself, had it not been for my children I would be dead today.

21. At least I never killed anybody or had an abortion. What about the baby killers?

22. There is no such place as hell. When we die we simply come back as something else.

23. There is no God. The government uses the Bible to control people.

Letter Eighteen
Knowledge

- My people are destroyed for lack of knowledge.
  — *Hosea 4:6 (KJV)*

There is a sad thing happening in the world today. Many souls are lost because of their lack of knowledge of God. The Bible warns us to beware of wolves in sheep's clothing. They are perverting God's words and leading many down the wrong path.

- Study to shew thyself approved unto God, a workman that needeth not to be ashamed, rightly dividing the word of truth.
  — *2 Timothy 2:15 (KJV)*

- But in your hearts set apart Christ as Lord. Always be prepared to give an answer to everyone who asks you to give the reason for the hope that you have. But do this with gentleness and respect. — *1 Peter 3:15 (NIV)*

It is crucial as Christians that we **meditate and study the Bible every day**. You must learn what the word of God says for yourself. There are tons of religions in the world. Some of which have their own Bible and their own teachings. Satan is trying to keep the true word of God hidden from man. The Bible refers to Satan as a thief.

- The thief comes only in order to steal and kill and destroy. I came that they may have and enjoy life, and have it in abundance (to the full, till it overflows). — *John 10:10 (AMP)*

- Jesus said to him, I am the Way, and the Truth and the Life; no one comes to the Father except by (through) me. — *John 14:6 (AMP)*

When you go to church, take your Bible with you. Attend Bible study and learn the word of God for yourself. The Bible forewarns us of false prophets in the last days. Engrave the word of God in your soul so that no man may deceive you. And take notes of the sermons you hear; check and see if they line up with the word of God. Pray for wisdom and understanding. Jesus warned us that in the last days, many false prophets would come in his name proclaiming that they are the Messiah and many will be fooled. Jesus has left us his word, which are his instructions during our time on earth. Everything we need is found in the word of God. The prophets who walked the earth before our time lived a life that was intended to encourage and strengthen our faith.

Reading God's word is not for entertainment purposes only; it is food for the soul. His word will bring knowledge into your heart that the world knows not of.

- Beloved, I wish above all things that thou may prosper and be in health, even as your soul prospereth. — *3 John 1:2 (KJV)*

- The fear of the LORD is the beginning of wisdom, and knowledge of the Holy One is understanding. — *Proverbs 9:10 (NIV)*

You are in a physical body, and you have a soul. Someday your soul will be required of you. Once your life on earth has ended, your soul will live forever. When you look into a mirror, the reflection that stares back at you is only a shell, or a covering. The real you (meaning your soul) lives inside your earthly body.

There are people who believe when they die they will be re-incarnated and return to the earth as someone else. Where is re-incarnation found in God's word?

In the book of Luke, there is a story written about a rich man who died, and opened his eyes and found himself in hell. Along with the rich man, a poor man named Lazarus also died. They each died, yet their souls ended up in two separate places. — *Luke 16:19-31 (KJV)*

We can walk around blinded from the truth if we choose to. According to the Bible, everyone will give an account for his own life on earth. If believing in the word of God makes me wrong, I don't want to be right. I would rather live for God and be wrong (according to the world) rather than risk dying without salvation.

There are many inspirational books written to encourage the believer, of course the Bible is the greatest book ever written. On the subject of ministers, not all ministers are ravening wolves. There are men and women of God who take their job of feeding God's sheep seriously. Studying the Bible on your own is fine, but it is equally important to attend church.

God has ordained certain people to be preachers, teachers, evangelists, and apostles. Their *job* is to teach you and give you more insight into God's word. "He who has an ear let him hear what the spirit is saying to the churches."

Letter Nineteen
I'm Too Religious for That!

Before I came into the knowledge of God, there were times when I did not feel worthy to be called a child of God. I pondered on my sins of yesterday as guilt and unworthiness filled my heart. Over the years, I visited many churches off and on, but I had not officially joined any. To be honest, some of the church members were downright overbearing. They spoke about the Bible as if they wrote it. It was nearly impossible to have a simple conversation with many of them. Every other sentence that poured out of their mouth was a scripture. I used to get so disgusted with their self-righteous attitude I wanted to throw up! I once listened to a woman quote a whole paragraph of scriptures to me. She was like a walking Bible. As she spoke, I couldn't help but wonder what planet she was from and what world she was living in.

I have arrived at my own conclusion in regards to churchgoers. There are two types of people in the church; there are religious people, and there are Christians. Religious people are very dangerous to be around; they are like inexperienced men with loaded guns. If they are not careful with their (words) weapon, someone may get (spiritually) killed.

Did you know religious people killed Jesus? They had lots of knowledge about scriptures and taught in the temple every day. The Bible refers to them as Sadducees and Pharisees. But when Jesus was standing directly in their sight they had no idea who he was.

When I was a kid, I used to wonder why the old ladies rocked from side to side as they sat in the pews. Sometimes they would get so filled with the spirit they would rise from their seat as the pastor preached. The old ladies had a look in their eyes that told of a great mystery. They had experienced Jesus in a way most people never had. If you would only listen, they would tell you all about the goodness of God. "God will talk to you and walk with you," they would say. I was curious about Jesus as I grew older. Would I ever know him like those old ladies that rocked from side to side in the church?

The average sinner will not go to church. Religious people sit back shaking their heads from side to side as they speak of how awful the sinner is.

- This is a faithful saying, and worthy of all acceptation, that Christ Jesus came into the world to save sinners; of whom I am chief.
  — *1 Timothy 1:15 (KJV)*

- But when Jesus heard that, he said unto them, They that be whole need not a physician, but they that are sick.

- But go ye and learn what that meaneth, I will have mercy and not sacrifice: for I am not come to call the righteous, but sinners to repentance.
  — *Matthew 9:12-13 (KJV)*

- An instructor of the foolish, a teacher of babes, which hast the form of knowledge and of the truth in the law.

- Thou therefore which teachest another, teach thou not thyself? thou that preachest a man should not steal, dost thou steal?

- Thou that sayest a man should not commit adultery, dost thou commit adultery? — *Romans 2:20-22 (KJV)*

- For not the hearers of the laws are just before God, but the ***doers*** of the law shall be justified. — *Romans 2:13 (KJV)*

- For all have sinned, and come short of the glory of God. — *Romans 3:23 (KJV)*

- Where is boasting then? It is excluded. By what law? of works? Nay: but by the law of faith. — *Romans 3:27 (KJV)*

Some people seem so holy you wonder if they can float. In God's eyes, we are all equally important to him. A self-righteous person might think he is above everybody else because he goes to church all week, holds two or three positions in the church, and can dance in the spirit even while the word is being taught. The church needs to set a better example. Is it no wonder why the sinner does not want to come inside?

Letter Twenty
Salvation

We are to display a *lively* hope (1 Peter 1:3) but lively or not, it is by *grace* are ye saved through *faith*; and that not of yourself: **it is a gift of God**: *Not of works, lest any man should boast.* — *Ephesians 2:8-9 (KJV)*

There is a lot of controversy about salvation. Some Christians believe once saved always saved, while others believe, you can lose your salvation. I try to stay clear of arguments about salvation. I only know in whom I believe. Everyone must work out their own soul's salvation.

- For I am persuaded, that neither death, nor life, nor angels, nor principalities, nor powers, nor things present nor things to come,

- Nor height, nor depth, nor any other creature, shall be able to separate us from the love of God, which is in Christ Jesus our Lord. — *Romans 8:38-39 (KJV)*

Paul states so beautifully in this passage that nothing can separate us from the love of God. I think it is essential we take note of the words Paul used to amplify his belief. Paul stated the words, 'things present nor things to come.' I interpret this passage to say even in my present life, or in my future, nothing can separate me from the love of God. When Paul spoke of depth or height, could he have been referring to heaven and hell? When I think of height, I think of heaven, when I think of depth I think of hell. Like Paul, I too am persuaded that nothing can separate me from the love of God. — *1 Corinthians 9:25-27 (KJV)*

Romans 10:9-10 states, if we confess with our mouth Jesus as Lord, and believe in our hearts that God raised him from the dead, we **shall be** saved; for with the heart man believes, resulting in righteousness, and with the mouth he confesses, resulting in salvation. Salvation is *free* lest any man should boast.

Before I finally accepted Jesus as my Lord and Savior, I went to the altar at least six times asking to be saved. People in the church had me so confused I did not know what to believe. It seemed that each church was preaching something different. The Baptists were saying one thing, while the Pentecostals were saying something else. No wonder so many people are confused today. I did not know what to believe. Therefore, I decided to learn scripture for myself, and trust in God's word rather the opinion of man.

Today there are masses of new churches opening up. We are no longer simply Baptists and Protestants. The Catholic Church has their way of teaching, the Jehovah Witnesses are saying their part, the Seventh Day Adventists are standing up for what they believe as well. There is just too much religion for me! We've got so much religion that people are forgetting about Jesus! I consider myself a non-denominational Christian. I don't label myself as being anything but a Christian. I am simply someone who loves God, and believes in Jesus and I am doing my best to one day hear him say, "Well done thou good and faithful servant."

Don't allow the world to keep you away from God. I wonder if he even cares what we call ourselves. The Bible says we perish because of a lack of knowledge. Let us not complicate the word of God.

There are those who live under the law, and those who live under grace. Nevertheless, do not be ignorant concerning God's word. Just because we are under grace that does not give us a right to sin. It is by grace we are saved. In the book of James 1:22 it states: "But be ye doers of the word, and not hearers only, deceiving your own selves." If you truly love the Lord you will want to please him.

Jesus asked a simple question that you might ask yourself:

- Why do you call me, 'Lord, Lord' and do not do what I say?" — *Luke 6:46 (KJV)*

Anybody can say they are a Christian, but if you look at their life, the way they treat people, and how faithful they are to God, you will know who they are. Jesus further added, in the book of Matthew 7:15-20.

- Beware of false prophets, which come to you in sheep's clothing, but inwardly they are ravening wolves.

- Ye shall know them by their fruits. Do men gather grapes of thorns, or figs of thistles?

- Even so every good tree bringeth forth good fruit; but a corrupt tree bringeth forth evil fruit.

- A good tree cannot bring forth evil fruit, neither can a corrupt tree bring forth good fruit.

- Every tree that bringeth not forth good fruit is hewn down, and cast into the fire.

- Wherefore by their fruits ye shall know them.

Your walk with God is something you will have to work on every day. He never said it would be easy, but knowing that he will never leave you offers quite a bit of hope towards tomorrow.

Do you think God saved us merely to just save us? He had a purpose in mind, and that purpose was that we would serve him, and become disciples for him. We must go out and spread the good news about the gospel of Jesus Christ. Luke 14:23 says that we go should out into the streets and compel them to come in. When I spoke of my feelings toward the backslider, I stated I had more respect for the backslider than for the man who never stepped out on faith.

Yes, salvation is free, but it came with a price. Jesus paid the price when he died on the cross. Accept the free gift of salvation if you truly want fellowship with the Lord. Jesus cannot go back and die on the cross all over again. His work on the cross is done. He has equipped us with all the tools we need to make it in this world. These are the final words of our Lord before he left his disciples and returned to the right hand of the Father. These words were not only for them, but for us as well.

Letter Twenty-one
The Final Letter

To My Beloved Sheep,

I know your deeds. See, I have placed before you an open door that no one can shut. I know that you have little strength, yet you have kept my word and have not denied my name. I will make those who are of the synagogue of Satan, who claim to be Jews though they are not, but are liars—I will make them come and fall down at your feet and acknowledge that I have loved you. Since you have kept my command to endure patiently, I will also keep you from the hour of trial that is going to come upon the whole world to test those who live on the earth. I am coming soon. Hold on to what you have, so that no one will take your crown. Him who overcomes I will make a pillar in the temple of my God. Never again will he leave it. I will write on him the name of my God and the name of the city of my God, the new Jerusalem, which is coming down out of heaven from my God; and I will also write on him my new name. He that has an ear, let him hear what the spirit says to the churches. — Revelation 3:8-13 (NIV)

All power is given unto me in heaven and in earth. Go ye therefore, and teach all nations, baptizing them in the name of the Father, and of the Son, and of the Holy Ghost: Teaching them to observe all things whatsoever I have commanded you: and, lo, I am with you always, even unto the end of the world. Amen. — Matthew 28:18-20 (KJV)

Conclusion

God is love. He is merciful, kind, and full of compassion, but he hates sin. The Lord wants to have a relationship with us because he loves us. Please take these **Love Letters from Heaven** seriously. I am aware that the world is busy; we are so busy that we don't have time to pray. Rather we choose to accept it or not, Jesus is coming back soon. When he returns there won't be time for excuses. If you have not accepted him as your Lord and Savior, please pray this prayer with me now. This is the prayer I prayed when I asked Jesus to be Lord of my life. Will you pray it with me now?

Dear Lord Jesus,

I realize that I am a sinner and unable to save myself. I confess my sins before you now, and ask for your forgiveness. According to your word if I confess you as Lord Jesus, and believe the Father raised you from the dead, I shall be saved. Therefore, I confess you with my mouth and I believe in my heart that you are alive today. Help me to walk upright before you. Teach me to live a life that is pleasing to you. I walk by faith believing that I am now a new creature in Christ Jesus and I take hold of your promise that you will never leave me nor forsake me. Thank you God for saving my soul in Jesus name. Amen.

Terri F. Williams

I'll Come When I'm Old
(A Prayer for Salvation)

God, I'm going to let you save me, just as soon as I am free.
But I've got to fix up my own life first, so I'll know how
things will be.
You see my problems are very big, and I hurt about them all
the time.
Lord, I'm going to make you proud of me, just as soon as I
make up my mind.
Besides, I'm too young to come now anyway, I've got my
whole life to live,
God, you understand what I'm saying? I know that you know
how I feel.
I'll come to you when I'm old, but I just can't come today,
Oh what a good person I'll be then, I'll even know how to
pray!
There are just so many Christians crossing my path, but what
am I to do?
After all I've lived a pretty good life and that should get me
through.
What is that sound I hear outside? It sounds like a trumpet
playing.
Dear God it can't be time already, if so you know I've been
praying.
Save me now Lord! I know you won't leave me behind.
Don't hold it all against me Lord, because I couldn't decide.
Here comes a little angel, he's come to take me home.
Save a seat for me Lord, next to your glorious throne.
But wait, he's going the other way, well I'm sure he doesn't
know,
That I'm supposed to be with God, not in the world below!
How could I have been so stubborn? Stubborn as a mule.
Thinking I was wise in my own two eyes, but playing the part
of a fool.
Maybe you can't decide and want to be like me, well you'll
find me in my cell, and you won't have to look very far my
friend, because my home is found in hell!

128

He's Got it Going On

God sees the problems in the world today,
but it's him man blames for his foolish mistakes.
And what about man, with his heart filled with greed?
When he prays to God at night, he says please God, please.
Give me all the things my arms can carry,
Send me someone to love, that I'll someday marry.
Give to me when I'm old and can't do any better,
and when my time is up, save a seat for me in heaven.
But when was the last time you put others first?
Forgot about your needs or your own hurts?
Or gave to a stranger sleeping on the street,
So they could have something nice and decent to eat?
All I ever hear is, "God is wrong!"
Well I'm here to disappoint you, because he's got it going
on!
Who do you think put the sun in the sky?
And make birds sing so sweet, it brings a tear to your eye.
What about the seasons? Yes, he changes the weather.
Now you have to admit it, God has got it together!
But all I ever hear is, "God is wrong!"
Well I'm here to disappoint you, because he's got it going
on!

The Writers

People say most writers are complex, and sort of hard to
understand.
We write about life and love, and beaches filled with sand.
We write about feelings that most people just can't express.
We can transfer feeling onto paper, so this separates us from
the rest.
We choose to dream, and live our lives just a moment at a
time.
Some of the most beautiful places that I've ever seen,
are embedded deep inside my own mind.
When I can't deal with reality, this reality we all live.
I get lost inside myself, and I write about the way that I feel.
I pick up my pen, and the words just seem to flow,
not knowing where they will lead me, or how far they will go.
Many nights instead of sleeping, I hold my pen in my hand,
as I travel through my own imagination, to some far away
distant land.
You see I do not write for glory, or to get anything for free,
I just sit down and I write, because it makes so much sense to
me.
I know after my life has ended, my writings will live on,
perhaps in a story, or maybe a sweet love song.
Because I do not write for glory, or to get anything for free,
I merely sit down and I write, because it makes so much
sense to me.

I Do

(Dedicated to the Military Wife)

A soldier's wife, not many can be,
She will keep her family together as he fights for the world to
be free.
Of all the wives in the world that have mourned, none can
compare with a wife in a storm.
Her feet remain unplanted as they move to some place new
For where he goes her heart will follow when she said the
words "I do"
The sacrifice she makes, she makes for life,
as she vows to stand beside him, as he goes off to fight.
Hear her voice, feel her pain,
for she is the strength that binds the chain.
She alone knows how hard it can be,
to lose a love so the world can be free.
Phone calls and letters must take his place,
until he returns, until they embrace.
The never-ending circle of love that she wears, declares to the
world that her love will never fail!
Through love and war she will remain true
For the vow she made will last forever, when she said the
words
"I do."

Author's Bio

Terri F. Williams currently resides in Michigan. She is the CEO and founder of Mrs. Bea's Publishing. Besides writing books, she also enjoys writing poetry, screenplays, photography.

Her current book "Love Letters from Heaven" is her second published book. Her first novel "Momma's Love" was the first of a trilogy. The novel was released in November of 2007. Due to an unfortunate accident, the trilogy was postponed. Williams plans to finish the trilogy, although at the present time in her life she states, "The Lord is leading me to complete this book before completing the trilogy." Her next book entitled, *The Biography of Shareé Miller: Daddy's Little Girl* is due for release in the spring of 2010.

While in college, she worked as a DJ for a local radio station in Knoxville. Williams soon realized spinning records was not her cup of tea. Writing was her true passion. During the late eighties, she wrote, produced and directed her very own show called the "Comedy Shop." The show was an instant success. A local cable station was so impressed with her writing and stage presence, the show aired for two consecutive seasons.

Today Terri F. Williams is an established author who someday dreams of seeing her work on the big screen. Williams quotes, "With God all things are possible. When my season comes I plan to produce major films and fulfill a lifelong dream."

To contact the author you may write to her at lovelettersfromheaven2009@yahoo.com. For book signings or public appearances, please contact publicist, Darlene House at the House of Communications at 313-778-1550.

LaVergne, TN USA
08 February 2010
172364LV00003B/59/P

9 780982 582107